# How To Be The JERK Women Love

## Social Sucess for Men and Women in the 90's

by
**F. J. SHARK**

Thunder World Promotions, Inc.
CHICAGO, ILLINOIS

**Additional copies of this book may
be ordered through bookstores
or by sending $12.95 plus $3.50
for postage and handling to:**

**Publishers Distribution Service
6893 Sullivan Road
Grawn, MI 49637
(800) 507-2665**

Copyright © 1994 by *Jerk School Incorporated*

**Publisher's Cataloging-in-Publication Data**

Shark, F. J., 1970-
　　How to be the jerk women love: social success for men and women in the 90's / by F. J. Shark
　　Thunder World Promotions, Inc. — Chicago, Illinios
　　　　　p.　　　cm.
　　Includes bibliographical references and index.
　　ISBN: 0-9640109-0-9
　　1. Interpersonal relations. 2. Men — Conduct of social life. 3. Women — Conduct of life. 4. Social skills. I. Title.
　　HM132.S53　　　　　1994
　　158.2 dc20　　　　　　　　94-70102

Manufactured in the United States of America

10 9 8 7 6 5 4 3 2 1

Text design by Heather Lee Shaw / PDS

*For Joel Blazek*
*& James Lisowski*

*Two friends of mine who left this world before their 19th birthdays,*
*and ahead of their own times.*

# *WARNING!*

## APPLY ALL INFORMATION CONTAINED
## HERE AT YOUR OWN RISK!

F.J. Shark, Jerk School Inc., Thunder World Promotions Inc., Straight Forward, Audio Images, ARS Recording Studios, Publishers Distribution Service, and all affiliations thereof, are in no way directly or indirectly responsible for <u>ANY</u> consequences, situations, or results you may encounter from the use of this material. By turning the page and reading this material, you fully understand this agreement, and hold no person, besides yourself, responsible for your actions.

Turn page at your own risk!

# Hey! Read This!

Believe it or not, I have the highest respect for women. Women can be the most caring, loving, committed, team players on the planet! The only problem is, sometimes they play for the wrong team! I believe that my material is actually benefitting women two-fold. First, it will take women inside the mind of the JERK to see just how he operates, as she learns some social self-defense (mentally and emotionally) to apply to her current and future encounters. Secondly, this material will make Nice-guys and girls a heck of a lot more fun, exciting, playful, spontaneous, adventurous, and maybe even a bit mysterious. By applying the strategies and techniques in this book, men and women can value each other as team players as they create more memorable moments in their relationships and hopefully put true JERKS and illegal drugs out of business because people will finally learn to get high off each other through positive emotional intensity rather than negative physical and verbal beatings.

*"Women are the Best Salespeople in the World!*
*A Salesperson's Greatest Challenges,*
*Mental Satisfaction, and Highest Emotional Highs*
*are Created from Making a Sale*
*to Those Who Were*
*NEVER Interested to Begin With.*
*This is Why the Customers that Don't*
*Look 'Hungry' Will Always Be Fed."*
*-F.J. Shark*

*"Expect more (good stuff), accept less (crapola),
and walk tall and kick butt with women !!!
Shark hits the nail right on the head!!!
This is a brilliant work that I'd require all men to read!"
-Ross Jefferies Author,
Secrets of Speed Seduction. . . How to
Create an Instantaneous
Sexual Attraction in Any Woman you Meet!*

**"I met Shark on the Montel Williams Show
and was struck by his laser like responses
to women who mistakenly believe that Jerks
do not attract women."
-Marcus Melton Author, Nice Guys Don't Get Laid**

*"Stimulating!
This book will certainly arouse
emotions in everyone.
Most will try and disclaim what it says.
As scary as it may sound, they can't!"
-Brad Braydon Owner, The Sultans Inc., Entertainment Agency*

**"The Shark speaks from the heart.
A man this wise is destined for greatness!
He has me thinking!"
-Mark "Body" Archer. Former Mr. Missouri and Mr. Mid-America**

*"Shark, I love the fact that you have
the courage to express your views
in your book. The opposite of bravery
is not cowardice,
it's conformity!"*
-Bob Croft, Mr. June in <u>*"The Fireman's Calender"*</u>

*"As the Chicago Bachelors Association's
Executive Director, I find that the Shark
has raised the credibility of JERKS to new heights.
His audio-tape program is clear,
articulate and humorous,
with a flair for intelligence—a must hear!"*
-E. Paul Jones Executive Director Chicago Bachelors Association

*"Why the heck wasn't Shark around
when <u>I</u> was 23 years old ?!?!?
Here's a guy who's caught on
to the mating game in its essence:
You can't have a successful committed relationship
with ANYONE until you're first committed to <u>YOUR SELF</u>. "*
*Jim Rohrbach, Social Skills Coach
Author of <u>The Social Skill Playbook </u>and recovering Nice Guy*

# Contents

Acknowledgements _____ 17

Foreword I _____ 19

Foreword II _____ 21

About the Author _____ 23

A Note from the Author _____ 25

Introduction _____ 31

1 - Play to Win _____ 35

2 - Learn or Burn _____ 39

3 - The Diamond Player _____ 45

4 - Love: The Most Expensive Illusion Know to Man _____ 49

5 - Antiphysics at its Finest _____ 55

*6 - The 2 Keys to Entering a Woman's Mind* _____ *65*

*7 - The 3 Most Powerful Influences of JERKS* _____ *71*

*8 - Expecting More* _____ *77*

*9 - Accepting Less* _____ *81*

*10 - Taming the Wild Wicked Ways of Women* _____ *85*

*11 - Selling Your Pickle* _____ *91*

*12 - The Social Sales Pitch — Who's Selling Who* _____ *99*

*13 - The Identity and Character Traits of JERKS* _____ *109*

*14 - Making Yourself a CHALLENGE!* _____ *119*

*15 - The 10 Commandments of JERKS* _____ *127*

*16 - The Gift that Keeps on Giving — NOT!* _____ *135*

*17 - Where this Book Really Begins* _____ *141*

*Exclusive Interview with F.J. Shark by  Ross Jefferies* _____ *147*

*Bibliography* _____ *153*

*Recommended Reading* _____ *155*

*Index* _____ *157*

# *Acknowledgements*

First of all, I would like to extend special thanks and appreciation to: **MYSELF** for gathering, learning and applying this information.

-To my family and friends that put up with my selfish, self-centered, egotistical personality and love me anyway for who I am.

-To the fake names and real people who are used in this book as examples of painful mistakes we can all learn and benefit from.

-To the millions of people like you that I have the privilege to share this socially sexcessful information with.

-To Carl's Photography for the Awesome job they did with the cover photo of this book.

-To Keith Medici and Borderline Productions, Inc., for the donation of the motorcycle.

-To Eric and Travis who were a part of our special wardrobe department and volunteered to help hold the exotic dancers' coats as they froze during the photo shooting.

-To all of the entertainers at The Sultan's Inc., including the two on the front of my book: "Alesha" and "Liza", two of the exotic dancers at Sultans and Kristin, an independent contractor/dancer.

-To the Vice President of Hot Chocolate - - my mom, who helped raise our body temperature in the 30 degree weather during the photo shoot.

-To Alex Moore at Publishers Distribution Service for Book Design.

-Special thanks for some statistics and figures gathered by: 365 Meditation, Reflections & Restoratives for WOMEN who DO TOO MUCH by: Anne Wilson Schae & 365 Days of Women 1994 Calendar Workman Publishing, New York

-Lastly, to the people that screwed us over and provided us with enough painful experiences to drive us to do something about it!

# FOREWORD I

*"Some men see things as they are,*
*and ask 'why?'*
*I see things that never were and ask,*
*'why not?'"*
*- J.F.K.*

**W**ell, yes. And smart men, like F.J. Shark, see things <u>exactly</u> as they are and ask, "what the heck can I do about it <u>right now</u> to get me what I want, when and how I want it?"

And <u>that</u> my friend, is what this amazing book you are holding in your hot little hands is all about: SEEING THINGS AS THEY ARE, not as you wish them to be. If you want to go on burying your head in the romantic sand, ( a perfect position to get your butt kicked), hoping against hope that one day a woman will come along who will appreciate your "niceness" (e.g. , your hunger and desperation), then you may as well put down this book. Go get something written by one of the "men's movement" authors. Or go to a therapist and "get in touch with your anger". Right.

If however, you are tired of getting the fuzzy end of the lollipop in your romantic encounters and are ready to start looking at and doing what <u>works</u>; if you're ready to get massive results by doing what women RESPOND to rather than what they <u>say</u> they want, then this book could well be the most important thing you will ever read. And the wonderful thing is that not only will you become fabulously more successful with women, but you'll also wind up liking and respecting yourself a whole hell of a lot more; a side benefit that is <u>not</u> to be sneezed at.

Just one more quick thing before I sign off on this foreword, and let you get started on this amazing adventure: invariably, when Shark presents his ideas on T.V. or radio, some idiot usually stands up and asks, "Why can't you just be yourself?" I hope you are not asking yourself that question, because what it really translates to is: "These ideas are too challenging for me to even consider. I'd rather sit here in my familiar prison of doing what DOESN'T work, and rot until I die, instead of having the courage to change." For God's sake I hope that isn't you. As you read this book, have the courage to go out and APPLY it's life changing ideas. The alternative is so ghastly that no one deserves it. Not even a feminist. Or even a self-styled "nice" guy.

Ross Jefferies
Master of Speed Seduction
Los Angeles, California

# FOREWORD II

In todays world, the battle of the sexes is taking its toll. Single people both men AND women, are scratching their heads trying to figure out how to get together with each other, and failing miserably. And wondering, "What's wrong with ME ?!?"

Enter F.J. "Shark", who has the antidote for all the confusion and despair. Refreshing as that first KER-SPLASH! in the pool on a hot summer day, he suggests to the men out there that they step out of the "Nice Guy" role they've taken on since the Stone Age ended and start treating women the way the women have been treating them-

LIKE JERKS ! ! !

Outrageous? Yes! Insensitive? Seemingly so! Abhorrent to women? ABSOLUTELY! I'll bet a lot of you reading these words at this very moment are somehow hiding the cover of the book from other's sight . . . that's OK! Perhaps you've been victimized by a JERK in the past. (Or, even BEEN ONE! - - Jerkdom does not discriminate on the basis of sex, race or religion.) Keep reading. Because beneath the bluster of Shark's bravado there's a genuine gem of a message:

STOP SEEKING OTHER PEOPLE'S APPROVAL–IT WILL ONLY BRING YOU HEARTACHE!

Yes, we're a society of approval-seekers. And women have used this knowledge on men for centuries - - the average guy will grovel at the feet of any attractive woman. This form of feminine manipulation has been a rather well-kept secret up until now. No wonder the ladies are crying "FOUL!" at the publication of

How To Be The JERK Women Love - - it blows their game ! ! ! Yet, if a woman were to carefully read this book, I GUARANTEE she'd be nodding her head in agreement at Most (if not all) of Shark's theories about male/female relationships. And she'd have a good laugh at herself as well as she recalled that the JERKS were the ones that usually wound up with her attention and affection!

But this book is truly for you guys out there who have allowed yourselves to be walked upon by women . . . when they've paid ANY attention to you at all. See, I agree with Shark - - you're never going to generate any interest from a woman until you give up your role as a pleaser and start pleasing YOUR SELF.

Read on with an open mind, enjoy, and tell me if Shark doesn't turn your head around. And discover that "JERK" really stands for "Just Expecting Respect, Kid!"

Jim Rorbach, Social Skills Coach
Author of The Social Skills Playbook
and recovering Nice Guy

## About the Author

"You'll see! Someday people from all over the world will listen to me, and use my so called: 'impossible and crazy ideas!' I don't know how it's going to happen, I just know it will!"
-F.J. Shark at age 17, responding to his family's disbelief in his first JERK ideas in 1987.

Since the above statement was made, F.J. Shark's social strategies and techniques have benefitted people in 4 countries around the world, and millions of people have seen and heard him interviewed on national television talk shows and radio stations across the country.

# *A Note from the Author*

**W**omen say I know too much. They are probably right! That's fine with me because I still find it utterly amazing that people from all over the world from virtually every walk of life seek out the social wisdom of a clean-cut, alcohol and drug-free, 23 year old Eagle Scout that at one point in time was the true definition of "socially bankrupt".

It's good to keep in mind that some of the world's wealthiest people financially were at one point some of the poorest. The spark that ignited them when they hit rock bottom financially was the same one found in me as I scraped along the bottom of the social marketplace. People who become successful with anything learn that success leaves clues. They learn from their own mistakes as well as modeling the actions of others until they learn the way the game is played.

Many of the people I knew in college earned straight "A's" from their first day in kindergarten, yet were rejected from the working market as well as graduate school. Myself, on the other hand, received a "D" in "Money and Banking", a 65% in "Finance 310" and an "F" in "Operations Management" and still had the $280 billion, #1 manager of financial assets in America offer me an opportunity in managing other people's money in the highest paying career in the world - - Stockbroker/Financial Advisor. The point is that you do not have to be a financial wizard or social guru in order to have the game work in your favor.

If you are at all like me, you do not want to wind up like the bald-headed beer-belly guy you see in a dirty white undershirt, eating pizza and watching football while his girlfriend/wife is out cheating on him in between bitching at him for something real or imaginary. The sad reality is that I have just described many of the unhappy relationships in the world.

So many guys think the social answer is money. Let me tell you the truth; money might get you marriage, but it says nothing about loyalty! If the ultimate fear is investing your heart and soul into a relationship and then finding out the other person is cheating on you with someone who is paying cheaper dues and receiving a better membership, then I submit to you that we start to model ourselves after the people who do the least and get the most.

Corporate America is a mirror image of the social marketplace. How many people do you know that work 2-3 jobs and gross under $25,000 a year in personal income? While on the cover of many national business magazines we find corporate presidents making well over $1 million for completing fractions of the physical labor that the average person invests.

Take a look at computer programmers. It's been said that the best computer programmers are the laziest. They do not want to type 100 lines of a program if they can find a way to get the same result in 50 lines. This act of laziness is the backbone of the entire computer industry. Every new advancement in technology is governed by the idea of getting a job completed in an even more impressive way with less effort, input and space. This is also smart business. The idea of keeping expenses (input) low and revenues (output) high is what businesses strive for as their goal. Therefore, it cannot be considered immoral, selfish, or wrong, to run your life with the same philosophies that have been the lifeblood of America.

To clearly see the tie in between the metaphors I use for the social marketplace referencing the big bad business world and stock market, you need to first accept the idea that not many people are going to help you in either one of these worlds. In fact, most people will do more harm than good by offering you what I call social smoke screens. An example of a social smoke screen is a person saying one thing and doing something else (i.e. women saying they want a "Nice-guy" and then going out with JERKS).

*"Never believe a woman,*
*not even a dead one."*
*-Old German Proverb*

It's been said that economics was originally called the study of the family. With this in mind, a family is like a business (having income, expenses, shareholders, etc.). Families are nothing more than relationships, regardless if they are good or bad. Therefore, the same types of examples and strategies used in controlling a business to the desired level of profitability can be used in controlling a relationship to the desired outcome as well.

I'll never forget the way I learned to watch what people are doing instead of just listening to what they are saying. My Father and I were in the middle of a snowball fight. He threw a snowball high into the air for me to watch as it was about to land close to me. Before the snowball was even on the ground, I was hit in the face with snowball #2. This simple distinction that I learned at the age of seven was enough for me to realize that I should be alert for what is really going on instead of just listening and focusing on what people want me to.

When you are driving, how do you know when the car in front of you is going to turn? The answer is when they actually turn! Haven't you ever been driving behind somebody whose turning signal has been on for the last 10 miles? It tells you that they are either thinking about turning or don't even realize that it is on. People are the same way about relationships. You should have as much faith and trust in the ideas that people tell you they are "going to do" or "intended to do" as you would the driver in front of you who seems to be going around the world to the left.

If I told you that a plane crashed, killing all its passengers, does that mean that we should throw away all the laws of aerodinamics and gravity? Therefore, if you apply these social sexess strategies to the laws of the Social Marketplace and it fails, does that mean the laws are worthless? All of these laws mentioned will remain constant long after we are both gone. You can either have them work for you by helping you take your life (plane) where you want to go, or you can crash and burn.

By modeling and living the strategies and techniques in this book, I submit to you that even the unpredictable social market-place will be as predictable as gravity itself. Gravity was here yesterday, it's here today, and you and I would be willing to bet that it will be here tomorrow as well. Success in anything from the stock market to relationships stems from investing in predictability. How in the world can we win a game if we don't even know how to play? At least women have magazines and themselves to network among as they compare notes on rela-tionship strategies when they experiment on their boyfriends with the social tip of the month. Most men around the world are completely out of tune to the mind games that women are playing in the social marketplace and therefore become an easy target, victim, and kill.

A very small group of men have figured out the game and are giving women a taste of their own medicine. They are called - - JERKS! My own definition of a JERK is someone who gets the maximum benefits such as respect and priority in a relationship for putting in the absolute minimum amount of time, effort and energy. It's been said that the word JERK stands for Just Expecting Respect Kid! Regardless if you are a man or woman that wants more respect and priority in your relationships, this book will help you from a social self defense (mentally & emotionally) to getting someone wrapped around your finger.

I personally believe that this book will outsell the Bible itself, because of the enormous market potential created by people caught between confusion and pain. That's the good news. The bad news is that it's been said that we live in a society that every 24 hours 950 people attempt suicide, ( 100 of which succeed), there are 40 new heroin addicts, 37 people die of alcoholism, and approximately 4,000 people experience their first mental collapse. Many of these tragedies can be attributed to people who bought into a bill of goods that said the more you give in relationships the more you get out. I believe, to an extent, nothing is further from the truth..The big bad social marketplace takes no prisoners and doesn't operate logically. Fortunately, it does operate with predictability. So we shouldn't ask ourselves if we can afford to learn a new angle on the social marketplace, but rather if we can afford not to.

# Introduction

*"If you listen closely,*
*you can hear the cries*
*of a thousand lost souls."*
*-Anonymous*

Did you ever read the "personal ads" in any newspaper in America? I do not view them as people trying to meet people, but rather as cries for help.

The numbers grow by the thousands everyday of those who add their name to the list of hopeless dreamers waiting for someone else to change their life and alter their destiny. If that is how desperate this country has become, we have an even greater deficit on our hands. With this type of social inflation, love today doesn't buy what it did yesterday and as a result, meeting places and dating services have become a multi-million dollar industry with no guarantee of satisfying results.

Nice-Guys are used and abused for their efforts and it is just a matter of time before they hear their girlfriend use the "F" word - - Friends! As used in the "nails scraping on a chalkboard" phrase: "Let's just be friends". Usually followed by plans of keeping in touch by talking on the phone the next time it rains or when the JERK she is going out with is blowing her off. There are really only two reasons why a woman would be in a relationship with a Nice-Guy: 1) Money and the concept of financial security, and/or 2) Being able to control him to meet her every want, need, desire and wish. If they say it is for <u>ANY</u> other reason at all, they probably lie about other things as well.

It's getting to the point now that I would support the idea of a guy going to pick up a girl for a date by saying: "Here is $30 for dinner, $7 for parking and $10 for the movie." Then give her a hug good-bye and still have time to catch the football game with his friends. I'm just kidding. Where in the world are you going to spend $10. for two people to get into the movies!

Now if there is one thing people are interested in, it is less effort and more rewards. The story of the prodigal son makes absolutely no logical or intellectual sense what so ever, but it still works to this day. That is the story of the two brothers working for the wealthy Father and one son decides to leave home and wants his share of the family assets. He squanders all of his money on good times and then returns home. The Father is so happy to see him that he decides to dress him in the finest clothes and throw a party. The son that was working hard all this time, reminds the Father that there was never a party for him and he is the one that has been working like a mule and obeying his Father's every wish. The Father tells him that his brother was lost and now is found. Meaning that everybody has the urge to go where they think the grass is greener. However, until you learn for yourself that it isn't, you will never fully appreciate what you had in the first place.

As far as the social marketplace is concerned, it is the story of the prodigal boyfriend. This is the guy that is really not comfortable with the idea of a serious relationship. He wanders off, cheats on his girlfriend, has tons of fun and returns to be just as accepted as he was before and possibly even valued more than a boyfriend that never wandered because she believes he actually found out for himself that the grass might be greener but it still has to be mowed. The hypothesis of being the best girl for him has now been tested through the fact that he decided to come back to what means more to him. This proves to her that her love for him is more powerful, strong and influential than any woman or good times he experienced on his little stray away from the relationship.

This is definitely a social handicap for people to communicate that they would never leave or hurt the relationship they are in because chances are that it has never truly been tested. The sport of bowling has a stupid handicap rule as well. This is where bowlers with lower averages gain points to assist them in winning the game. It seems the worse off your average is, the more benefits you receive and less effort you need in order to win. This is also true in the social marketplace and why:

*"The new law of social America*
*is survival of the <u>unfit</u>;*
*Nice-guys are becoming social dinosaurs*
*because they are not reproducing."*
*-F.J. Shark*

# 1

## Play to Win

*"Nice-guys finish last."*
*-Leo Duroucher*

**WHAM!** Jim's fist smashed into the wall unlocking a reservoir of frustration and pain which only he had built up inside. As usual, it was too late for his emotions to explode and the only one that he was hurting and cheating was himself.

His so-called wife had taken full advantage of another situation and created a series of arguments just before storming out of the house with their child, leaving Jim embarrassed in front of his own family, stripped of his pride, and raped of his manhood.

She had mastered and played his hot buttons like a professional musician on her instrument. This was definitely not the first time nor would it be even close to the last time an ego crushing experience would enter the relationship and sting Jim right where it hurt. It was obviously clear that he was emotionally and socially poor, well on the road to a destination of mental bankruptcy.

Every single effort of love on Jim's part went unnoticed,

unappreciated, and eventually thrown away like a cheap free sample you get at the grocery store. Trying to talk about problems in his relationship was like throwing good money after bad into a failing business that has so much momentum on the downward spiral that every second you sit on the edge of your seat clinching the armrest with complete uncertainty, except for the fact that you are destined to crash and burn.

After re-evaluating his past actions, Jim put the blame on life itself, that he was dealt a bad hand in the card game of life. He now believed it was just his job to accept it all in stride. It seemed to make sense. After all, he was a caring and loving husband, supportive Father, cooperative and helpful son, nicest friend you could ever have and a shrewd hardworking entrepreneur that provided more than enough for his family. He had always met his wife's every wish, want and need, yet seemed to come up empty handed and unrewarded for his efforts.

Even when it seemed Jim was winning all the battles, he would still lose the war. For example, when he was in his dating stages, he believed that being well liked by his girlfriend's entire family carried with it some magical powerful influence. I guess this was his idea of an insurance policy. In the event of a relationship ending argument, this weak prayer would bring her back because her family would talk her into it by reminding her of all his good points. As if it actually mattered to be admired by her parents as the type of guy they wanted for their daughter, best friend to the potential brothers and sister-in-law, while being approved by the grandparents as "This is the one!" And not only able to put up with and find the good in that uncle nobody likes, but also trusted by the dog as one of the family. If these statements were true, the type of boyfriends brought home that parents have nightmares about, would never receive a second date.

Sadly enough, this is where a Nice-guy would pay the dues and this type of Jerk would be receiving the membership in any relationship for minimal efforts of input while being rewarded with the maximum benefit package consisting of respect and priority among everything else a woman could offer.

I'm not being negative, I'm being accurate. I wish we lived in a world where we are rewarded for being courteous, generous, kind- hearted people, but the reality is that we don't. The reality of the social marketplace is how it is, not how we wish it was. The horrifying truth is that we live in a world where every 6 minutes a woman is physically attacked, every 3 minutes a woman is raped, the average married couple speaks to each other 4 minutes per day, and most people have already figured-out that the more you give to a relationship, the less you receive.

How many times have you seen someone more socially successful than you who seems to put in a very little effort (if any at all) and reap the social rewards most people dream about? What makes some people gain respect and priority as they abuse the unfair advantage they have while others are treated like a consolation prize and continue to lose the social shell game? Were some people provided with special 3-D social glasses in order to see what others can't? At one point in time, somebody came up with the phrase: "It's better to have loved and lost than to have never have loved at all." What does that mean? That makes as much sense as: "It's better to have driven off a cliff than to have never have been in a car."

Why would anybody be concerned about being nice? Being nice is like the cover page of a term paper or extra credit worth only 10% of your final grade. The point is that your term paper, final grade and relationship can live without it. Why bother doing a 10% extra credit project if you never did any of the other work? Why bother spending the majority of your time on the "cover page of your life" when people are primarily interested in being a part of a juicy adventure story. If you make your life exciting and adventurous enough, people won't care about your "nice cover page", as long as they can get on your team, and be a part of the memorable, intense fun and action that they will tell their grandchildren about.

But don't worry, everybody knows that "Nice-guys win in the end." What end? Marriage? At least that's what women want you to believe as they are running around having intense fun with Jerks until they want to settle down with a Nice-guy to flip the bill for security in her life (i.e. house, car, and children) when the party is over. This is equivalent to a sports car having miles put on it and then when the motor is shot, find another owner that you can go a little slower with and won't know the difference anyway now that the good times and partying stages are over. Now, unless you like going around after parties are over and finishing what people didn't drink, and eating the left overs that fell on the floor, I suggest that you find a way to get invited to the party when it starts.

In other words, you must either . . . .

# 2

## Learn or Burn

*"Winning is a habit; unfortunately, so is losing."*
*-Vince Lombardi*

**IF YOU** are sick and tired of getting sick and tired with women, then you came to the right place! Relationship pain is at its all time high in the social marketplace. It seems people are only interested in the fun and excitement, yet nobody has time for the pain of working out problems.

Remember the TV show "The Love Boat"? The captain would greet everybody at the door and wonder who he is going to be entertaining for the rest of the evening while somebody else was steering the ship. Women are the prime example of this with what I call the "Authority Without Responsibility" attitude, which is equivalent to wearing the captain's hat and not steering the ship in a relationship. They want the power and control in the relationship, but most of them expect the man to handle all the work while they can focus on having a good time and not be responsible for any consequences.

Did you ever notice the elephant at the circus that was tied with a tiny 4 foot rope? The reason for this is that when the elephant was younger, ( and smaller), it was tied with a similar rope. It pulled and pulled on the rope till finally it gave up and never tried again to this day when it weighs a few thousand pounds more. The elephant will never question the strength of the rope again because of what it was taught to believe.

The old-fashioned core belief of the social marketplace is that the social universe, including all men's individual worlds, faithfully orbited around the most powerful center of gravity - - Women! This is comparable to the Geocentric model of the universe which stated that all the planets revolve around the earth. Sadly enough, for hundreds of years, people believed in this way of thinking to the point of being punished, tortured, and even killed by their government and religion if they even questioned its truth. Fortunately, for all of mankind, a few courageous astronomers did not accept this belief and observed for themselves what was really going on and came up with the Heliocentric model of the universe which places the sun in the middle with all other planets orbiting around it.

Our parents made the mistake of teaching us good little boys to grow up and be responsible polite gentlemen, treating women with special velvet gloves, and always putting their wants, needs and desires ahead of our own in order to keep them happy. I experienced enough social pain in my life to come to the conclusion that our parents were about as right as the governments and religions that supported the idea of the Geocentric model of the universe. Don't get me wrong. It's not that our parents were out to harm us. The fact is, our parents were giving us the best information they could with the resources they had. They probably received the same information from their parents and grew to believe it with complete acceptance without ever questioning its truth like the elephant or the people of the

Geocentric Age.

With enough social pain to drive me, I set out to do something about the package of social beliefs that I was sold. My quest for such profound knowledge attracted me to an Anthony Robbins seminar called : "Fear into Power, the Firewalk Experience!". This was a weekend seminar including the virtual act of walking barefoot on 12 feet of 1,800 degree coals of fire. (Do NOT try this new picnic skill without the correct supervision of professionals, (i.e.. people crazier than you!)). The seminar taught me such things as: If you want to be healthy, then study health. If you want to be wealthy, then study wealth. Therefore, I thought if you want women, then study women and the Jerks they love. Every woman I know desires Rock'n Roll musicians who are either on MTV or playing at a local nightclub. How many times have you seen women literally throw themselves at some unattractive, skinny, unmannered, financially poor musician who couldn't care less if she was alive?

These Rock'n Rollers all share the same common denominators of beliefs and actions about women and about what comes first in their own life. The bottom line is that musicians can get as much sex as they want from as many women as they want by putting the least amount of effort and energy into any relationship with women. The purpose behind this book is to model the most socially successful people and increase the amount of women in your life while decreasing the amount of effort on your part.

Some of you will respond and pick up on this material like second nature, while others will have to make some adjustments, like my '81 Camero that had its spark plug wires mixed up. If you think of it, at one point in time, tying your shoes, a simple magic trick and riding your bike, all seemed next to impossible until you learned some simple distinctions and practiced a specific strategy. So put on the training wheels and follow this social sexcess recipe. If you stick to the game plan (i.e. social sexcess recipe), you will find truth in the old saying: "If you do what you've always done, you'll get what you've always gotten."

Did you ever see how a movie is made? I had the good fortune of going to Universal Studios in California where they take you behind the scenes to show you the Hollywood special effects that are not shown to you at home. It seemed simple only after you saw how it was done. Magic carries with it the same type of mysterious illusion until you see how the trick is performed. What I intend to do is take you behind the "Social Scenes" and show you the social tricks men have been falling for, as well as that "Man behind the curtain" like in the movie "The Wizard of Oz". The frightening truth is that you will find a woman behind the curtain pulling strings, pushing hot buttons and creating all the special effects and illusions that we are not supposed to question, because: "Women have spoken! Hear them roar!". Most women are a bit concerned that I am blowing their social cover as I introduce techniques, strategies, and beliefs that were only found in the "girl talk" at slumber parties, national female magazines and tacky romance novels, but that just tells me that I am on the right track.

Sexcess in the social marketplace does not involve phases of the moon, luck or even Hollywood special effects; it comes from mastering the social fundamentals. Did you know that in order to achieve the rank of Black belt in Karate, you need to master 8 basic moves? Did you know that the association that creates the A.C.T. and S.A.T. college tests have openly admitted that there are only so many formulas to give examples of? There are only so many green trains leaving for Los Angeles traveling 69 miles per hour that will meet a red train going to Chicago at 66 miles per hour. The color of the trains, their origin, destination, or speed are completely irrelevant if you know the correct formulas that will allow you to plug in the numbers and complete the problem. I understand that people are all unique and should be treated like individuals. However, there are certain social patterns of input and output that need to be mastered. Mastering them would provide you with the unfair advantage of a student who has the answers to the test they are about to take. Not mastering them provides you with the painful reality that I was right.

Certainly the one person who has a true unfair advantage in the Social Marketplace is . . . .

# 3

## The Diamond Player

*"Women are like dogs;
the more you beat them,
the more they love you."
-Words of a convicted wife-beater*

*IT WAS* 5:30 A.M. Sunday morning. My family and I sat with great anticipation to hear my voice come through the radio from an interview that was conducted weeks before on Chicago's most popular rock'n roll station.

The young listening audience for miles and miles were probably just staggering in from Saturday night. To our surprise, the show that was played right before mine was about wife-beating. "Oh, this ought to be good!" I said sarcastically. I thought to myself: "Who was the marketing guru that put a show about wife-beating right before they bring on the president of Jerk School Seminars, Inc!" Luckily in my defense, when I was interviewed, I mentioned that I do not support the idea of physically abusing women, nor does any of my material relate to pick-up schemes or juicy one liners that every women is just thirsting to hear. I also was willing to admit that I have never used illegal drugs or even drank alcohol. Sadly enough, most of the Jerks that have women wrapped around their fingers fit the description of drug, alcohol and girlfriend/wife abusers.

During a live interview with people calling in, I remember a specific woman who obviously called in to voice her lack of support for my Jerk ideas. Sensing that the listening audience was going to be on her side if I didn't do something quick, I immediately began to think of a way to turn the tables on her and regain my credibility. Instead of yelling and screaming at her, I simply asked her a few questions and threw her completely off balance. I asked her what the average length of a relationship was that she had with the boyfriends that were Jerks. She said that they lasted about 2-3 years. I quickly asked her how long she had ever gone out with a Nice-guy. She said that it was about 2-3 weeks at most. I then said: "Case closed! Next caller!"

Women will tell you all day long about the qualities they want in a guy, yet they will never go out and have fun with someone that meets that description. Women are even willing to admit that it is stupid to go out with Jerks, but they still do. Most women involved with Jerks actually feel useful because they: 1) have a sense of being needed, 2) have a chance to defy their parents like a naughty little girl or 3) prove people wrong on the idea that he is not such a bad guy after all.

It seems that Nice-guys are the health food of the social marketplace because they are good for you and have no taste. Jerks, on the other hand, are the junk food that everybody knows is bad for them, but they get eaten anyway. Any candy and junk food manufacturer in the world has a much easier time selling their product over health food because the junk food people can excite you on the fun and high levels of intensity as they splash the flavors on the screen and show people having a good time in the process.

You are a product in the social marketplace and you have a choice. Either have your product sit there on the shelf as people go past and tell themselves that they will start that diet next week or you can be the product that gets purchased.

> *"Nice-guys are on the shopping list going into the social marketplace, but they are not in the grocery cart coming out."*
> *-F.J. Shark*

Wanting my product, (myself) to have a great demand in the social marketplace, I began to act more and more selfish with a myopic, uninterested view toward relationships. The strange thing was, the more uninterested and selfish I became with women, the more women would be waiting in line to spend their boyfriend's hard earned money on me and sell me on the idea that relationships can not only be fun and exciting, but one of the best long-term investments of my life - - NOT!

In a short period of time I became that one guy they couldn't control, that one guy every girl wanted because nobody could have him - - it was awesome! I considered myself to be a "Player" in the social marketplace and it felt like the cards of life had dealt me 4 Aces. I thought I was on top of the world as girls would sooner please me rather than their own boyfriends, who were paying the dues while I was exercising the membership.

Well, if you live by the sword, you should expect to die by the sword. One girl that I was actually in a relationship with (and started to fall for) brought to my attention that she wanted to see someone else and couldn't make me any promises about the future of our relationship. She said, and I quote: "Ya see, it's like if you've got crystal and you've always desired a diamond, you go for it if you get the chance!" This is the point at which most people on this planet would consider jumping off of a building, crawling under a rock or start to feel sorry for themselves as their heart had just been smashed into a million pieces - - Not me! To this day it amazes me about what I said to myself after she left my apartment. I yelled: "Wow! Holy Sh-t! That's powerful" I began thinking: "How could some guy come along and just take over a relationship that actually had some substance to it? How did he create such a powerful influence in such a short period of time? How could he win against me? After all I'm the one with the 4 Aces!"

Later I learned that in poker, however rare it may be, a Royal Flush beats 4 Aces any day. From that moment I wanted to be the hand that wins across the board. Why bother with other combinations if you can have the one that takes over in a heartbeat? What I am talking about is becoming not just a Player, in the social marketplace, but a DIAMOND PLAYER.

The first thing a Diamond player learns is the definition of . .

# 4

## *Love: The Most Expensive Illusion Known to Man*

*"It is ridiculous to think you can spend
your entire life with just one person.
Three is about the right number."*
*-Clare Boothe Luce*

**WOULD YOU** invest in a business franchise that had a 50-60% failure rate, 70-80% of the investors disappointed on the return on their investment, and 30-40% of the investors openly admitting to cheating on their business partner? Then why do millions of people invest in the most frustrating, disappointing, unrewarding and costly business in the marketplace - - Marriage (still the #1 cause of divorce!).

Have the 80 million single people in this country gone absolutely out of their mind? Especially men. I know why women want to get married, but guys should ask themselves what can they get out marriage that they can't get out of a dating relationship. Sex, closeness, or even being part of a family do not require a legal documented contract called a marriage license.

If you think of it , all of the above would probably even lose some quality and value through a marriage relationship. The only thing I see a guy gaining from marriage is something called Alimony!

I'm not blaming women. If I were a woman, I would do the exact same thing. Let's see, if I were a woman, (F.J. Sharkette) I would have as much fun intense emotional highs as I could with as many wild and crazy Jerks as possible until I was in my mid to late 20's. Then, I would start looking for a Nice-guy that went to college, had a well paying career and control him through sex to meet my every want, need, desire and wish. (Sound familiar?) After about 5 years I would divorce him by saying: "I just don't feel the same way anymore. You understand, don't you?" Mr. Nice-guy would probably suggest family counseling and reading some "Love Doctor's" book, (who is afraid of risking his/her reputation by revealing the truth), in order to save the failing marriage. He would learn things like drawing a line down the middle of a piece of paper and working out our differences. After he bored me to tears, I would cheat on him with his best friend, and take Mr. Nice-guy to the cleaners for everything he's got! (Does it sound familiar now?)

Most of these "Love Doctor's" books preach about being understanding, caring, trustworthy, loyal, helpful, friendly, courteous, kind, obedient, cheerful, thrifty, brave, clean and reverent. (That old Boy Scout Law just won't leave my mind!). The authors relay their boring information in a very passive way, by telling us all what we want to hear. They accomplish this through the stale conditioning and repetition of telling us that: "Tomorrow is another day", and we should remain hopeful while we are wishing for things to get better in our relationships. The key distinction between those books and mine is that they tell you what you <u>want</u> to hear, and I tell you what you <u>need</u> to hear! I do not feel sorry for the 'social victims' regardless of sex, because I believe in the social marketplace, "There are no victims, only volunteers." Haven't men been hurt enough by women striking at their egos by saying that they don't make enough money to keep up with the Jones's? The Grandma's of yesterday are becoming extinct and the new social evolution has given birth to a breed of woman that proudly screams: "I am a woman! Hear me roar!" Women are now thinking for themselves and most guys aren't thinking at all. It's been said that the larger a woman's breasts are the less intelligent she is. I submit to you that the truth is: The larger a woman's breasts, the less intelligent the guy becomes.

In the everlasting fight for equality among the sexes there are too many inconsistencies to the equation. I strongly believe that society was made to benefit women in the first place. Take a look around from divorce settlements to "Barbi" having "Ken", while "G.I. Joe" had nobody. It's perfectly acceptable for 2 women to dance together if they can't find a partner and not for men.

*"Never trust a good woman,*
*and avoid the bad ones."*
*-Chinese proverb*

Other classic coincidences that are a catch 22 perfectly set women up in "win/win" situations such as:

-Women want men to make all the plans on a date by being

prepared, but if he does, she complains that he did not consider her feelings.

-A woman will get mad if a man is 15 minutes late to pick her up for a date, but she can keep him waiting 45 minutes while she finishes getting ready.

-Women say that if a man gets lost driving he is too macho to ask for directions, yet if he does, she thinks he is a stupid idiot.

-If a man offers his seat to a woman on a bus or offers to help with a physical task, he's sexist. If he refuses to help, then he is not a gentleman.

-Women object to words like: "businessman", "chairman", and "mankind", yet I've never heard one complain about the phrase: "women and children first".

-Women want an ambitious, successful man, but complain when he can't spend time with her because he's putting in the long hours of success.

Women want a man who treats his mother well. Once they find him, he's called a mama's boy.

-If a woman wants to date a few men, she is exploring new options. If a man does this, he is afraid of commitment.

-Many women object to taking the man's last name when marrying because it is an outdated and degrading tradition, but they do not object to tradition when a man spends two months salary on a ring.

-When a woman wants to have sex, it is a beautiful expression of her love. When a man wants to have sex, he is a sick pervert. And my personal favorite:

-When a woman puts down men she is a woman's libber who is fighting for the rights of all women. When a man puts down women, he is an insensitive Jerk!

If I were to die and become reincarnated, I would want to come back as a beautiful woman. As far as sex goes, I do believe Ross Jefferies, author of the book: <u>How to Get the Woman You Desire Into Bed,</u> when he said: "For men, sex is a chore, and for women it's a choice." Think about it - - smart women can sit around all day and watch soap operas as they think about which one of their boyfriends they will let please them tonight.

What's this P.M.S. stuff? No, it's not "<u>P</u>utting up with <u>M</u>en's <u>S</u>h-t!". It's more like: <u>P</u>-ss and <u>M</u>oan <u>S</u>yndrome! Once a woman knows that you are addicted to her, the P.M.S. starts a week early, lasts more than a week, then flows into "Post Menstrual Syndrome". This leaves less than one week for sex with you, which she spends out with her girlfriends looking for a more challenging guy. You, in the mean time, are busy wondering if "Miss October" really does care about planting trees in the desert. To fight back for the equal rights of men around the world, I have come up with some P.M.S. that guys can use to even the score. It stands for: <u>P</u>re (and <u>P</u>ost) <u>M</u>onday Night Football <u>S</u>yndrome" which starts on Friday night when we go out with our buddies and continues well on through Wednesday as we discuss scores and complain about plays that should've happened while we jump up and give each other high fives and yell out the name of the hottest girl at the office. With this type of crazy social insight, you should have no trouble at all understanding the meaning behind . . . .

# 5

## *Antiphysics at its Finest*

*"Less effort creates more results."*
*-Unknown*

CROWDS STINK! Looking around at an exciting amusement park on a sunny day, you see the faces of disappointed and frustrated people who have come to the realization that thousands of other people had the same idea - - to show up today as well.

I remember walking toward the exit of the park recalling all the fun intense highs from the day - - roller coasters to soaking wet water rides - - that my friends and I took part in. However, I was continuously interrupted by the bitching and outspoken complaining of most of all the other people around us. All I kept hearing was: "I can't believe we waited 3 hours for a 30 second ride!" and "This sucks! I spent $26 to go on 2 rides and wait in line again for expensive food that was tasteless!" My friends caught wind of the complaints and asked me: "Were these people in the same park as us? How were we able to go on all the rides we wanted (some twice) and had no lines for lunch?"

The answer was simple. When the park opened and the majority of the people went for the most popular and newest rides, we were going to shows. While other people were going to lunch, we were on the newest rides. When other people were going to shows, we were eating lunch. I purposely suggested ahead of time that we do the opposite of everybody and my friends had no idea the value of this information until the day was over. This belief that the "masses are asses" holds true in both the stock market as well as the social marketplace where the big picture is playing - - Life!

Any amusement park or similar example is like a microcosm of life itself. You will have winners, losers, and people wondering what the game is all about. I'm here to tell you that there are not too many women breaking down the door of a nice-guy who plays his life according to the masses and is like everyone else in his need to be accepted.

Two guys can go out with the same woman (even at the same time) and get treated completely different. As a result, it seems she is happy when she is with the Jerk, who becomes like an addictive drug that she cannot get enough of, and complains to her friends about how he mistreats her and reminds her of how boring they (her friends) have become. On the other hand, Nice-guys are used as emotional teddy-bears that have to spend their time planning how to entertain her like a court jester trying to make the queen laugh. In the meantime, she looks forward to going out with her friends, who are more exciting than he is, and hopes that the other mysterious, unpredictable guy will call her who is more fun than all of them put together.

Jerks and Nice-guys are about as far apart as you can get on the social spectrum. Nice-guys appear to be next to perfect. I have news for you: If a woman cannot get any attention from her friends by complaining about your negative points, she will look for one or even make some up if she has to. If you believe that she will brag to her friends about how great you are to point that you will be fighting them off and making her jealous because your demand is going up - - you are wrong my friend! I'm not saying this type of action never works, I'm saying that I like to put the odds in my favor and play greater percentages that have a more meaningful impact in order to make a lasting impression.

If you have many faults up front, which she recognizes (being late, canceling dates, blowing her off, etc.). then believe it or not, as she is complaining to her friends about you, what is going through their minds is that they can be "the one to tame you" and reap the rewards for themselves. It's like the cowboy that makes a comment about a mustang by saying: "I just can't break him, he's too wild!" The other cowboys know the rewards of being the one to break this mustang that everyone is talking about getting thrown from.

### *"The one who loves the least, controls the relationship." -Unknown*

Nice people must want something. Did you ever notice that even when we were younger, our parents sensed when we wanted something simply because of our hungry actions? How did you treat the last person who was "overly nice" to you? Did you feel they were up to something or trying to take advantage of you and insult you intelligence? Well, didn't it occur to you that women can pick up on this as well? Strangely enough, if you are continuously showing her that you are not interested in her by treating her with disrespect, then you are not a threat to her freedom and are not trying to get or take anything from her by manipulating her.

## "Those that don't look hungry get fed."
## F.J. Shark's Golden Rule of the Social Marketplace

If you do not appear to be hungry for a woman then she will think that your needs are being taken care of somewhere else and surprisingly enough start believing: 1) You are a disinterested prospect in her product and therefore she can turn you around and sell you on the idea of becoming an interested lead that might wind up kissing her ass. 2) If you are ignorant enough, she will take it upon herself to try and change you for the good of all society. And 3) Accept you as a challenge because you probably have a girlfriend and there are so very few things a woman considers more exciting than the thrill of the hunt and capture/steal of another woman's man. This proves that her product (beauty) and sales-personship is more powerful than some other woman's on the planet.

If you can't seem to "keep the fires burning" in a relationship, it's because you are using the wrong means at the wrong time. The way relationships start can be compared to starting a forest fire in the woods. If you start with a big log (too much at at one time) you will never get it lit, much less even have the chance to keep it burning. This is just like the Nice-guy who brings and offers too much to the relationship and snuffs the flame. The Jerk, on the other hand, brings very little, like kindling that is easy to ignite and then the girl is the one that keeps adding the emotional logs to the fire in order to keep him interested in the hot, spicy, burning relationship. As she is doing all or most of the work in the relationship, the last thing on her mind is to cheat, because she doesn't have time to even look for somebody better, or leave the relationship because she has so much invested and needs to get something out of it. Now she is the social entrepreneur throwing more good emotion after bad, as she decides to go down with the failing and sinking relationship because she has so much time, effort and energy invested.

Considering there is no such thing as a "Love collection agency" in the Social Marketplace, the only way for her to collect the love she put in is to be around him long enough until he decides to do something loving for her for a change. The Jerk, by this time, is keeping a roving eye open for some new girl because this one is considered to be "no big deal" in his mind due to the fact that he was given everything in the relationship for free, and that is the exact value he has on it.

Would you appreciate a team sport if they didn't have try-outs and everybody made the team? How would you feel if they gave away all the trophies and awards on the first day for no reason? Athletes around the world put the greatest value on the events that cost them the greatest amount of focus through the high level of competition it offered. On the other hand, if you received your awards and trophies on the first day, why bother showing up for the rest of the season? Nice-guys are a prime example of this by giving a girl free credit by trusting her too soon in the relationship and volunteering to become her slave for any work she needs to have completed that is interfering with her having a good time today. The girl links up in her mind that if she did nothing and got rewarded for it, why bother changing her strategy and invest any emotion if she gets it all for free.

Ever go to the "Auto Show" in your city? I am usually at Chicago's Auto Show every year and it amazed me especially last year when the auto industry was having some difficulty selling cars and the salespeople at the show were more eager and hungry for a sale than ever before. It was like a three ring circus, watching all of them fight to capture your attention so that they can hand you a bag full of information and tell you about their special financing and great deals with cash back if you buy their car today. As I walked around I noticed the exotic car collections which included Rolls Royce, Ferarri, Lamborghini, etc. . These cars had few salespeople and had most of the people standing in awe as they dreamed about one day getting behind the wheel of one of these incredible cars. I thought for sure that with the economy in sad shape and the prices of these cars so high, the manufacturers would be offering special deals on them. To my surprise, there was no bag full of information, no high pressure salespeople and not even an attractive and flashy display around the cars. Out of all of the exotic cars I only noticed one that had a sign which read: "At 207 m.p.h. who needs a philosophy?!" Meaning, they are not going to give you a special deal or sell you on the new door locking system in the car. They realize that if you desire the emotional highs bad enough that this car has to offer, you will find a way to afford it. This selling strategy also keeps the general public financially out of reach, which makes these cars even more rare and special.

If you think this type of arrogant attitude stops at the trade show you are wrong! I really wanted to get a brochure on a Lamborghini, so I drove to one of the dealerships. Thinking again that if this is where most of the sales take place, it would make sense to offer some information considering they are asking for

10 times more money than the average car on the street. The salesperson said that they did not have any information on the cars because their image sells themselves. They are also in no hurry to sell you one of their cars and feel if you cannot afford it, then keep your nose pressed up against the window and dream on!

If you have to continuously sell your girlfriend on why you should be going out together, you are doing the both of you a disservice by creating the same cheap feeling people received when they heard the pitch of the hungry salesperson at the Auto Show. This will result in her believing in the old fraudulent mail order saying: if it sounds to good to be true, it probably is.

" One of the greatest key distinctions between Nice-guys and Jerks is - - fear of loss. The Jerk has no fear of loss of the girl he is with because: 1) he knows there is an abundance of girls on the planet that he has yet to conquer, and 2) he has probably had better than the girl he is currently with or at leasts gives her that impression by keeping a roving eye open for someone better.

I believe there are 3 stages in a relationship with comparison to Nice-guys vs. Jerks. Stage 1 is introductory where the Nice-guy believes that he needs the woman to make his life complete and because he is so hungry, he is willing to pay what ever price she asks. The Jerk, during stage 1 is not hungry and doesn't need her for anything because he probably has more women than he can handle now. During stage 2, the Nice-guy is convinced that the woman is the best woman he has ever gone out with as the Jerk is convinced that he has had better. By stage 3, the Nice-guy is stuffed and mounted as an easy kill as he communicates to the woman that she is all he ever needs and the Jerk is telling her through his actions that she is not enough. These 2 completely different strategies can send you in opposite destinations such as the difference between being the consolation prize and being the most valuable person in her life that she can't wait to see you again.

A fork in the road is started at a single point. What path you decide to go down is determined in a moment and then grows further apart as time goes on.

*"In your moments of decision,*
*your destiny is shaped."*
*-Anthony Robbins*

One key moment that decides your social destiny is as simple as how you ask a girl out regardless if it is the first or last date. If you want to go the the movies and bring some girl, the way you ask is a key factor in the path you are about to journey down. The conversation between the Nice-guy and a potential date would be something like: Nice-guy (N.G.) says: "Cheryl, do you want to do something this weekend?" Cheryl: "Like what?" N.G.: "I don't know, maybe like go to the movies or  something?" Cheryl: "What's playing?" The Nice-guy will read her the entire list of movies at 3 different locations and wait for an approved response. This is your first step down the path to the destination of being an approval seeking wimp that will be wrapped around her finger by the end of the evening (if she does decide to go out with you and nobody else is around to have fun with). This approach gives her too many options to pick from and too many chances to cancel out. The Jerk's conversation would go something like this: Jerk: "Cheryl, I'm going to see XYZ movie at 9:30 tonight. Do you want to go with?"

Cheryl: "Oh Yes! I was hoping you would call. I thought you forgot about me!"

The rest is history. This approach quickly gives her the impression that you know what you want, you're going after it (the movie), you have a busy schedule, and you are going to have an awesome time with or without her. Even if she cannot make it for whatever reason, you have given her the impression that seeing the movie is more important than seeing her and you will proceed to call the next girl in your little black book. You are the one in demand and she has the opportunity to have a good time and jump on your fast moving "train of fun". Now she can be just a ship in your harbor instead of being the harbor that your ship wants to get into.

We all agree that you need to be a little different in order to stand out in a woman's mind. Therefore, in order to unlock the door, you need . . . .

# 6

## *The 2 Keys to Entering a Woman's Mind*

*"Where the mind goes, the body will follow."*
*-Unknown*

**SHE WAS BEAUTIFUL.** Standing there with her hair in a ponytail, moist lips and a sexy body that was hidden by the retail store's smock that she wore at the check-out counter, this girl had been complimented by literally hundreds of guys a week that went through her check-out lane. My buddy and I were figuring out what to say to her when it was our turn for her to ring us up. After we both said: "Hi!", the next words out of my mouth were: "Do you ever wear your hair without the pony-tail?" She said. "Yeah, why?" As I got my change I said: "Because it would look a hell of a lot better than it does now!" and walked away. She was so shocked to hear something other than a compliment come out of my mouth that she even thanked me in a sincere tone of voice for telling her as she agreed with me. My buddy was trying to keep from laughing because he knew what I was up to.

We both went back the next day simply to see if she changed her hairstyle and sure enough it was without the pony-tail. We got in the next line over from hers and when she saw us she said smiling: "How's that?" I said: "Well, as a rule I like pony-tails, but with your outfit neither of the styles look attractive or sexy." She asked me to wait until she was finished with the current customer, who by the way, was a guy complimenting her on the way she looked. After she took his compliment and put it on the pile with the others in her mind, she said to me that she was getting off work in 10 minutes and would like my opinion on clothes she was going to try on at a different store in the mall. I agreed, but only if she would hurry because I had somewhere to go. (Home, to laugh my ass off!)

With respect to my time, she pulled me along the mall into the store she wanted to go into and I immediately suggested some other store because something just wasn't right about the image of the store in relation to her. She bought it, and we went to two other stores that I suggested. I spent the next 45 minutes granting approval to some of the sexiest dresses on one of the hottest bodies I had ever seen in person.

Do you think I would have had that much influence on her if I was complimenting her like everyone else did? It was not luck or being in the right place at the right time, which so many people base their entire social growth on. It was a simple bit of contrast that set me apart from what she was used to. In the Social Marketplace, there are 2 types of women: 1) Premiums and 2) Discounts. Premiums are over-priced (usually social and emotional rip-offs) that walk around with their nose up in the air and expect everyone to kiss their ass. They have an attitude, a highly inflated price and high maintenance because all their life people have been handing them compliments. And if you hand her one, she will add it to the pile. Discounts, on the other hand, have not been complimented that much, and as a result, have lower self-esteem. When you compliment them, they will fully appreciate it because they are not used to any one paying any attention to them what so ever.

Remember how hard you worked in school to receive something like: History C+ Algebra D+ Phys. Ed. A English B- What did your parents notice first? They certainly did not fully appreciate the "A" in Phys. Ed.! They focused on the "D+" in Algebra because it stood out as a poor grade. I know people who received straight "A's" with one "B" and their parents had to sit them down to lecture about the quality of achieving good grades and bringing up their grade point average. I also knew people whose parents worshiped a "C-" and "D's" because there were no other passing grades on their child's report card. Everyone's parents focused on what was different because it is built into our nervous systems to spot contrast the same way a wild animal notices an uncamouflaged prey through the process of natural selection.

To better understand how this example ties into the Social Marketplace, go get a regular deck of playing cards. Choose one complete suit from black and a complete suit from red. For the sake of this example, let's have the black cards represent the bad/negative comments a person might hear about themselves, and the red cards represent good/positive comments. Line them up in order of their value so that you have one black row and one red row at opposite ends of one another. For example, the red king, (strongest compliment, i.e. "I Love You"), should be to the far left with a continuation of the red cards going right until the red two, (weakest compliment). The next card should be the black two, (weakest put-downs), continuing to the black king, (strongest put- down, i.e. violent argument or physical abuse).

The girl at the store was definitely a Premium that has had mainly high red cards in her self-esteem portfolio. Usually, when a person has too much of something, they take it for granted because it was handed to them for free, there is a lot of it, and more is on its way in. This is why my 6-7 black card put-down was what she focused on. I was somebody who didn't pay her "suggested retail price", and further acted like I had seen better. In order to remain congruent in her own mind, it was her job to sell me on the idea that she was beautiful. The clothing store is where her mind was saying: "Here! Do you find me attractive now? How about now? How about now?", as she would try on dress after dress. The women that are wrapped around a Jerk's finger can literally spend a lifetime trying to please him and gain his approval for their beauty being the best thing he has ever been with (as a result, very few succeed). The ones that do succeed at getting the actions of the Jerk to represent that she is the best and most beautiful woman he has ever been with (i.e. commitment and remaining loyal as he gives up his other passions in life to make her #1), usually get dumped, or at best get a lower quality of relationship with a higher price for him to pay now that he realizes her value. She will probably start looking for some other guy to change, who is a harder sell and not as easy a kill.

Beauty is a leading indicator to whether a woman is a Premium or a Discount. However, the deciding factor is how she views herself. It's great to have strong self-esteem and be beautiful, but those alone do not qualify someone for the Premium status, because some unattractive girls have the biggest attitudes, and some pretty girls honestly do not recognize the value of their own beauty as being something special.

The logical solution is to find beautiful girls that have an undervalued view about themselves. There is one tiny problem. Nobody wants a girl who does not know how to handle a compliment regardless if she is beautiful or not. The reasoning behind this is if she is so easily swayed by someone else's opinion, you might have quite a job standing guard over her 24 hours a day because she gets weak in the knees if some guy starts flirting with her. One time I heard an interview on the news with a prostitute and she said: "I am the perfect woman or wife for a man because I know how to please him and I know when some other guy is hitting on me, so I can turn him down." What more could a guy ask for?! The secret in having the greatest amount of impact on a Premium or Discount through the use of contrast is to remember a phrase of mine which states:

> **"If you want to have an impact
> in the Social Marketplace,
> treat the Premiums like Discounts,
> and the Discounts like Premiums."
> -F.J.Shark**

After you master the art of identifying the difference between Premiums and Discounts and getting on their minds, you can start to have an even greater impact once you use . . . .

# 7

# The 3 Most Powerful Influences of JERKS

*"When you are as old as I, young man,
you will know there is only one thing in the world
worth living for, and that is sin."
-Speranza Wilde, Mother of Oscar*

**THE NEXT TIME** you get into an argument with a woman, what are you going to do? Follow one of those "Love Doctor's" advice and take out a piece of paper, draw a line down the middle and list your differences? - - NOT!

I do not believe any relationship in the world is 50-50 and you are always going to have differences. The closest it can be is about 60-40, to as far down as 99-1, which is the puppet on a string. To whatever degree of influence you want in a relationship, stick to my fundamentals of S.I.N. which are the 3 most powerful Influences of Jerks.

**S**pecial: Create moments for yourself and others that will remain with you even on your death bed. Do what most people don't do, stray from the path and create the fun of intense

71

adventure. Don't be normal! Make your dates extraordinary by going on a ghost hunt with a professional ghost hunter ($22 per person), rent a snowmobile or a jet-ski ($40 per hr.), slide down a giant water slide, or just ask yourself: "Where is the craziest most outrageous place we can go right now?" Be spontaneous! Remember, she can get anybody to sit on their ass at home and watch television with her! By doing fun, exciting, spontaneous, adventurous, unpredictable things, you will be known as a fun, exciting, spontaneous, adventurous, unpredictable person who is definitely in demand in the Social Marketplace and one girls never forget.

*"The only difficult part on stage
is making it look spontaneous."
-A Rock'n Roll musician*

**I**nterest: Not sexual interest. I'm talking about asking her questions about herself and what she likes to do for fun. Compliments should be given sparingly so that they are appreciated. Never give a woman a compliment on any part of her physical beauty too early in the relationship. Small compliments about clothing, jewelry, perfume are appreciated only if they are done without flattery and routine.

**N**eeded: What's the first thing a doctor asks the patient in the hospital? "Where does it hurt?" Women can be the best doctors in a relationship by making you feel better and work on taking away some obstacle that is in your way, providing she is a Teamplayer and knows where you need help. Don't wait for them to ask - - tell them! You do not need to make things up or rely on B.S. because nobody's life is perfect. You can certainly find something to complain about in your life that she can help you with, can't you? It is amazing what people will do if you just ask them to and let them "try-out" for being a member of your team. Never need a woman for fun. You should be in 100% control of your own fun and therefore have a monopoly on it. The last thing you want to have happen is that you are dependent on her in order to have a good time to the point that you cannot enjoy the moment you are in at the time. This will lead to the price of your fun going up and the quantity and quality of the fun she decides to throw your way will begin to depreciate.

Don't feel guilty that she is helping you for free because she isn't. She simultaneously is, like the old saying, "Tuned into W.I.I. F.M." radio, which stands for: What's In It For Me! If you reveal what your passions (hobbies and fun activities) are and ask for help with them, don't be surprised if you sense that through her actions she wants the same strong feelings you have for them to transfer over to her. Beware! Her first step is to eliminate your idea that you are so passionate about, and replace it with her. - - NOT!

In the stock brokerage industry, like all businesses, if you are not taking care of your clients, then somebody else is. If women are more than willing to offer you their help by you simply asking, you would be a fool not to use it. Someone once said: "If you are not using it, you are losing it!" You are only cheating yourself out of someone helping you and cheating them out of the gift of giving to you. Don't treat women like that special cologne that you never wanted to use because you were always saving it for special occasions. After a few months you will notice that the cologne has evaporated and so has your woman. If you reject her help or don't even ask, she will either openly offer it to some other guy or be that much more willing to go help anybody that she can find so that she can simply feel needed or a part of a team.

Can you name one of the most popular, fastest growing social clubs in America today? The answer is - - Alcoholics Anonymous. Some say it is due to the rapport of the people sharing the same problems. If so, then how do you explain the sober women that go to the meetings just so that they can meet men? Women stay alert for undervalued assets and unpolished gems. At these meetings, they can buy them at a tremendous discount (on sale) and gain the capital appreciation when the stock/person is back to its full market value. For example, if a stock/person is $50 a share and you invest $1,000 you will get 20 shares. If the stock goes up $5, it is a 10% return on your investment leaving you with $1,100 ($100 profit). However, if a stock/person is $5 per share and you invest the same $1,000 into it, you will receive 200 shares. now if the stock goes up $5, it is a 100% return on your investment leaving you with $2,000! ($1,000 profit!). If she is an astute investor and owns what society considers to be such junky, low quality stocks/people then she will have her hands full as she tries to prove her friends and family wrong by selling them on all his good points which nobody else seems to see. The only reason she sees them is because her mind is blocking out all of the bad (black card) parts and she is focusing on the few good (red card) parts.

Women actually believe that if they help him get his life together and turn him into a winner, he will owe her what she wanted in the first place - - loyalty and peacefulness from a man who was possibly considered to be dangerous once he was drunk and now is tamed and will never throw her off again. After all, if she did all that for him - - "How in the world can he even think of leaving the relationship or cheating on her?", which are coincidentally her two greatest fears. This is why my Jerk School Seminars are co-ed offering women - - "How to be the Women Men Stay With."

Using influence is one of the main factors in the Social Marketplace that you either have or you want. This chapter prepared the foundation for the ability to be. . . .

# 8

## Expecting More

*"There are two fools in every market:
one asks too little, one asks too much."
-Russian proverb*

**HOW TICKED-OFF** you would be if you found out that your girlfriend used to give her ex-boyfriend foot massages, home cooked meals in bed, money that she worked hard for, and more sex in a week than you receive in 6 months?

Don't look so surprised. These are probably ALL true! There is no reason to get mad at her because you are receiving much less for a greater price than Mr. X had to pay because there is nobody to blame but yourself. Yes, you!

I have news for you. If you are not the selfish one in the relationship that makes requests about every little need, desire and wish that you want done for you, then you are in trouble. Remember the old phrase: "If you don't know what you want, someone will know what they want you for."

Would you ever go into a restaurant, sit down and expect them to feed you exactly what you wanted without you even placing an order? Or go in and say; "I'll have whatever!", and actually look surprised when "whatever" comes your way? Even if you tell them you want steak and it comes out charcoal well done - - it's too late! In the Restaurant of life, you have to not only place your order and tell people what you want, but you have to tell them to what degree you prefer it.

Most Jerks have great expectations of what they want a woman to do for them, and that is one of the reasons why they get women to do almost anything for them. The next time you hear about some woman helping a Jerk in anything from washing his clothes to planning and paying for a romantic get-away to Mexico, it is the result of what the Jerk expects the woman to do in the relationship (i.e. his order in the Restaurant of Life).

Remember that teacher you had in school that had such great expectations for the class? He/she had very demanding assignments in which you had to make special time out of your day just to finish the extra work. She also outlined for you exactly what effort it would take on your part in order to receive the grade you wanted. You probably knew on the first day of class what it would take to receive an "A" in that teacher's class. You probably had to cut other classes or miss other assignments from other classes in order to finish what you had put so much time, effort and energy into. Telling people what you like only helps them please you. If you are not supplying a woman with enough light in your darkness then don't be surprised if she decides to grope around in the dark with somebody else as she looks for the switch to "turn him on."

It's true. Don't rely on her to know exactly what you want, need, desire and wish. If you asked her about those things mentioned at the beginning of this chapter, I bet you she would either admit to them, or lie to you. If you asked her why she doesn't do such sweet things for you, she will come back with: "Well, you never asked me to!" After you are finished gritting your teeth and punching the wall because of all of the moments you missed in the past, focus on the only thing you have control over - - the moment you are in now! It's been said that: "The past does not equal the future." So, the simple fact that she did more in anyway for some other guy is at least a sign that she can do more for you than she is doing now. Think of about 10-15 ways she can do more for you. A good place to start is by asking her what she did for other relationships in the past. If she doesn't want to talk about it, then take my advice and believe in the saying: "Whoever keeps their mouth shut about certain things, must have an awful lot to hide."

Don't value what you get as much as you value what she has to give. Some women offer more of themselves (time, emotion, finances, etc.) simply because they have more to give. Girl #1 that gives you 9 out of 10 = (90%) of her life is giving more of herself than girl #2 that gives you 20 out of her 100 = (20%). If a similar example gets brought up to you by girl #2 who says: "I gave you more than twice as much as your other girlfriend did, so, therefore, you should love me twice as much!" - - NOT! If she gave 20, than she can give 40, because she probably gave the last guy 80 which still doesn't add up to girl #1's 90%!

There are many lessons to be learned from expecting more from women and this chapter provided you with the training wheels necessary to get you started on your way to . . . .

# 9

## Accepting Less

*"It's a funny thing about life;
if you refuse to accept anything but the best,
you will very often get it."
-W. Somerset Maugham*

*I COULDN'T WAIT* for try-outs. Our high school track team was nothing to write home about, but I was excited about being on a real team representing my freshman class. After a few days of running around like crazy, I found out that there were no "cuts" from the team. Everybody made the team, as long as they were willing to show up. I immediately lost all respect for the team and cut practice on a frequent basis because I not only wanted something that was going to challenge me, I wanted to feel special in the process. I wanted to feel that others wished they were in my shoes and the reason I was in my position on the team was because I was good at it, not picked at random. This thrill weighed more than the sport itself!

In the big bad business world and the Social Marketplace, being "All things to all people," is the formula for failure. A real estate billionaire once said: "If I got involved with every deal that landed on my desk, I would have gone bankrupt years ago." Success in anything comes from being fussy about what you spend your time on, and who you spend your time with.

The social paradox is what makes the socially rich get richer and socially poor get poorer. If you accept to go out and do something every time any girl asks, you are slicing your own throat. Because even if you are seeing 3 girls at the same time, they will begin to think that you have nothing better to do and nobody better to do things with. You need to be the first round draft choice for her fun, not the consolation prize she calls because she knows you will be ready and waiting to do anything with anybody. Make sure you get the leading role when it comes to fun, and never accept anything less.

**"I would rather be first in a small city in Gaul, than second in command in Rome."**
**-Julius Caesar**

Don't accept her bitching either. If she wants to continuously bitch about her family, friends or broken nail, then do yourself a favor and leave now. There was a story about a helium filled blimp that was breaking away, and some of the men that were pulling it down were now lifted off the ground. The ones that let go when the blimp was 10-20 feet off the ground at most broke an ankle. The ones who let go at 100-200 feet or higher fell to their death. Don't fall to your social death by hanging on to someone who is not a team player. Or worse, they are a team player, but they're not playing for your team! If they are more of the cause of problems than solutions, then they will actually benefit you more if they are playing for another team. If they are interested in complaining and bitching, then let them find a Nice-guy to listen to them because he has nothing better to do. He will probably think she has an interest in him, and there might be sex later (and he might be involved) if he just provides good listening skills now. Don't worry, he will turn into her emotional teddy-bear or big brother, and that is exactly how she is going to kiss him! In the Social Marketplace, people will step on you for as long as you let them.

> *"If you are constantly being mistreated,*
> *you're cooperating with the treatment."*
> *-Unknown*

Women love to test guys and see just how far they can push them. I call this process the: "Jackass" test. They are going to dish out as much crap as you can tolerate to see what it takes to make you mad. The next time you feel that you are being put through this test, wake up and remind yourself that this is America, and there are plenty of choices available to you. In other words: "YOU DON'T HAVE TO TAKE IT!" Not here, not from her, not from anyone! The bitch that you bring out of her can only live and exist with the power you give it. I call it the "Demon Bitch". It shows up ever once in a while, and then disappears because it realizes that it has no power.

*"Nothing has any power over me other*
*than that which I give it through*
*my conscious thoughts."*
*-Anthony Robbins*

If you are unsure about what to do in the situation, just ask yourself: "What would a Jerk do?" Or better yet: "What would a woman do to benefit from this situation?" The conclusion that you will come to is that you need to say "No" in a relationship more than "Yes". For example, I remember when I agreed to go and pick up my girlfriend during her half-hour break at work. This was the second time I was doing this and realized that we didn't even have a chance to be alone together last time because she went in the kitchen to talk with her mother and I settled for playing video games with her younger brother. This time, when she got into the car, she said: "Well, are we going to go to my house?" I said: "No, we're not!". She looked at me with a bit of confusion, and then I told her that I did not intend to spend our "Quality time" laying on the floor playing video games with her brother, while she talked with her mother. I'll never forget the look on her face as she said that she was impressed that I wanted to be with just her and I was not going to settle for less. This was not for Marriage, it was for a measly 30 minutes, and look at the impact and difference the word "No" made. Remember, JUST SAY NO, when you are dealing with women, or any other addictive drug!

With the right amount of influence on your side, through expecting more and accepting less, it is now possible to start . . . .

# 10

## *Taming the Wild Wicked Ways of Women*

*"Nature has placed mankind under the government of two sovereign masters: Pain and Pleasure . . .they govern us in all we do, in all we say, in all we think. "*
*-Jeremy Bentham*

**DID YOU KNOW** that the penalty for drunken driving in some countries is death at sunset? Would you be more likely to drink and drive in that country or one that suggested a $10 fine? As long as you are aware of the law enforced by death, during the deciding moment of getting drunk, most people would choose not to.

So why do some people flirt and cheat outside their relationships? The answer is simple - - lack of respect and value for the other person. Broken down, the word respect means: re: again and spect: to look at. Therefore, true social respect is to "Look at again" or review what you could lose in the relationship. It makes you focus on the level of pain your mind will go through as a consequence of your actions. The decision itself takes less than a second. The jury, in anyone's mind, votes if this action is worth the pain it might go through later. In other words, how valuable you believe the original person you're considering cheating on is to you, and what the consequences are for your actions (i.e. how fast you can get off the hook providing you are caught) will ultimately control your decision.

Remember that teacher who really got mad and punished the students if they didn't do their homework, or that coach that yelled his head off when you were a few minutes late for practice? Their subject and sport probably had the top priority in your mind over other classes and extra activities at school. What character trait did that teacher and coach have that the others didn't? Yes, they Expected More and Accepted Less, but they went a step further. The step the other teachers and coaches were lacking is one of the greatest differences between Nice-guys and Jerks - - They got MAD!

All teachers sold us on the idea that studying would lead to eventually getting a well paying career. This type of positive reinforcement works about as well as a Nice-guy constantly reminding his girlfriend that if she stays with him now, the rewards and benefits later will be great (i.e. well-paying career and financial security). The teacher who reads you articles about how poorly the economy is doing, and how difficult it is to get into a good college so you can have a better selection of companies to work for will have a much greater chance of influencing you to study because he/she is using the painful thoughts of not being accepted at the college of your choice and being left behind in the job market in order to motivate you. It's been said that pain and pleasure are the only two motivating forces, and sadly enough, pain moves us quicker because it is a survival mechanism built into our nervous system.

Every class for every subject you ever took in school had one key moment where the students would either respect or defy the teacher for the rest of the year. The first time the teachers boiling point was reached the students were testing the limits of what they could get away with. This is the key moment. The level of noise, for example, is beyond what the teacher is willing to accept and the students are keeping one eye on the teacher to see his/her reaction. If the teacher decides to deal with it in a calm cool manner or blow it off, he or she should hand in their resignation now and avoid the cost of future shock therapy treatments he/she will need because of a nervous breakdown!

The only choice the teacher has to save his/her own mind and respect from the students is to get MAD! This could come in the form of writing out detentions to screaming at the class and throwing a chair across the room (with a student still in it). What works long term is something that jolts them, something they will remember the next time they realize they are pushing their luck over the limit. The important point to remember here is that the "mad" actions must be carried out and not just talked about or used as a threat because it would be the equivalent of never having them to begin with.

The only reason people are afraid of or at least handle grenades and other bombs with a great deal of care, is because they know what damage could be done it it explodes. Even by accident the bomb could explode, so therefore people are extra cautious regardless if they have intentions of using the bombs or not. In relationships, the person that gets more respect is the same person that gets mad easier and quicker ( shorter fuse on their explosion), not to mention the more intense. I call this person the "Madable" one because they demonstrate the ability to get mad and explode their emotions at the drop of a hat. Guess what? If you are not using the Madable Theory to your advantage, then it is using you.

*"The secret of success is learning*
*how to use pain and pleasure*
*instead of having pain and pleasure use you.*
*If you do that, you are in control of your life.*
*If you don't, life controls you."*
*-Anthony Robbins*

Being Madable is an awesome way of reversing the "Bitching Technique" used by women, that men all around the world have suffered for. The reason why guys get "whipped" is because the woman constantly complains and criticizes while the guy is busy trying to make her shut up by running around and meeting her every want, wish, need and desire. The guy actually feels that if he does as he is told and carries out her wish as his command, there might be sex later and he could be involved. It gets to the point where women have power of attorney (complete disgression without question) over the guy's mind. He does not even question what actions she wants him to do for her as long as she doesn't start bitching and the option of sex later remains open.

Women have set up what I call an electrical social fence around the yard of the relationship. If you stay in the yard and the boundary of the fence, you are safe. However, even touching the fence and testing the limits brings with it an electrical shock that zaps you with verbal and emotional voltage to let you know where the boundaries are. The sad part is that the yard keeps shrinking as she tries to gain more control over your decisions; turning you into an approval seeking wimp that just has to worry about the next way the queen wishes to be pleased.

The people on this planet will only appreciate the good inside of you if they see the bad come out of you. In other words, they won't respect and value how good it is, until they experience how bad it can be.

### *"You have to experience the night so you can appreciate the day."*
### *-Unknown*

Would you invest in a company in the stock market if the price kept reaching new highs every day? If you are an experienced investor, you would say: "No, because the faster and higher some stock rises, the faster and harder it crashes." It is better to look for companies trading at a discount that have experienced the all time lows because they have no where to go but up, and at least it can't get any worse than it is.

### *"In the world of relationships, when you are at the South Pole, every direction is North."*
### *-F.J.Shark*

The most astute social investors in the world (women) need to know one thing before they invest any of their emotional, sexual, mental, financial and social capital - - What is the downside risk? How bad could it get? Nice-guys never get MAD and as a result women wind up not trusting them because they are considered to be phony due to their lack of being real, which includes getting mad - - a way to show that you are human. In the stock example, stocks go up, stocks go down. People are the same way. They have their good days and their bad days. By not letting people experience your bad days is like a company in the market that never wants to reveal a down tick on their stock. You think you are doing your investors a favor by not having your stock drop a few points (letting them see you get mad), but they will take it as an insult and sell their investment in you and go someplace else as they wait for you to finally pop and drop (sometimes crash and burn), due to all the pressure, frustration and anger, you built up within yourself which was never released. It will eventually explode, maybe even for no apparent reason, like that bomb that just explodes without warning or intention. None the less, I can promise you that your girlfriend won't be around to see it, because who in their right mind would want to hang on to something if they had no frame of reference about what it was capable of doing. Even the women that are physically abused in relationships know how bad the beatings can be, so therefore by not revealing your mad intense feelings in a relationship is like a stock without a chart of its history. I'm in no way advocating physical abuse, but my point is: How can people learn what good is if you give them nothing to compare it to? In the Catholic Bible, even doubting Thomas and Judas the Betrayer come across as more appealing than the devil himself!

This chapter explained why 99.9% of women do not cheat on

Jerks and can be summed up in 2 key points:

1) Jerks are Madable with painful, explosive consequences (emotional, social, mental, sexual and even physical) that have a very short fuse. 2) The girl is so busy meeting the Jerk's expectations and pleasing him by doing things that would NOT make him MAD that she doesn't have any time to cheat or even keep a roving eye open for somebody better.

Once people have experienced the Madable side of you, investors (women) will begin to buy into you and your stock because you just crossed the line from a good company to a good investment. With the increase in your own demand in the Social marketplace, you will now need to learn how to be more effective at . . . .

# 11

## Selling Your Pickle

*"Caveat emptor: let the buyer beware."*
*-Business Law term*

**PEOPLE** are influenced by price. At the neighborhood deli, there were two jars of pickles with different signs on top of each. One read: ".89 ea.", the other read: "$1.39 ea.". When I asked the butcher what the difference was in the pickles and why someone would pay more for one pickle that looked like every other pickle, he said: "They are the same pickles, but some people feel they just want to pay more for quality, that's all."

If you are interested in buying a product you are not familiar with and intend to keep for a while (i.e. new CD player, fax machine, etc.), you'll usually judge the level of quality by the price of its competitors. This results in purchasing the higher priced item due to the saying; "You get what you pay for." We do this with people as well. If we are not familiar with somebody we will see what kind of price they have on themselves. By price, I mean: Their level of self-respect that they have for themselves and what they expect people to "pay-out" (emotionally, mentally, socially, financially and sexually) in order to afford them. If you have a high level of self-respect then most people will automatically treat you with a high level of respect as well. Unfortunately the opposite is also true.

Nice-guys fall prey to this because they are too good a quality for their discounted price and as a result any girl can afford them. In fact, she can probably afford 4-5 Nice-guys for the price of 1 Jerk. Nice-guys have low cost, low maintenance, low impact, and low value in a girl's mind. Nice-guys think they are doing women a favor by keeping their price so low because they know women like things on sale. Somebody forgot to tell Nice-guys the other part of the saying: "Women like expensive things on sale." Negotiating for a slight discount on a Lamborghini is exactly what I am talking about. Most people would feel they got a special deal if they bought a $300,000 Lamborghini for $269,000. The bottom line financially is that you paid more than 10 times the average price of a car that has the same four wheels touching the ground as any other car. A Yugo is also a means of transportation so how come everybody doesn't want one if they are so affordable?

Remember, nobody "needs" a Lamborghini. People want, desire and wish for them. It's been said that if a society bought only what it needed, it would collapse. The key question is: "What makes people willing to buy such expensive products if they are completely aware of cheaper ones?" The answer is - - Image: perceived value.

A wise old salesman once told me, "What the customer thinks it's worth is much more valuable than what it is really worth." I took his simple advice and went to a well known retail store in November and bought 5 Christmas pins that were in their own individual little boxes for $1.99 ea. . The next day I went to work and told people I was selling Christmas pins for $4.00 ea. . The first two people I approached bought all 5 and asked me how many more I had. I started writing down orders from people who were literally throwing money at me saying, "Get me 2 Santas, 1 Christmas tree, and 4 bells with the ribbons on them."

Women are the most emotionally, socially, mentally, sexually, and soon to become financially wealthiest people on the planet. With this kind of abundance sitting around in social silos and sexual reserves, you would be crazy not to get a higher price for yourself, regardless of what it is now.

If you have the right price on yourself, women might buy into you, but what makes them come back for more? The same thing that keeps the cigarette, alcohol, and drug industry profitable--Addiction! The illegal drug industry alone is a $100 billion + empire. The reason is not because they have such great sales-people, but rather (sadly enough), it makes people feel good through mental and emotional highs. I submit to you that we should model and sell ourselves the same way drugs are sold. The first few encounters with you are free, with no obligation. Then the price goes up. Soon, it costs more and more money, (time, effort, and energy from the girl), to buy more and more of the drug (you), to create less and less of a high than the time before. The intense state of mind that the person is in causes them to think about nothing else except the next high (date) with the drug (you). **The addiction comes from not having the drug.** If you are easily accessible you will never be in demand in the Social marketplace. Cutting your supply (time you spend with her) will automatically increase your demand (time she spends thinking about you) and allow you to charge any price you want because by now she is an addict of your intense fun and desires nothing more than to "get high" off you again as soon as possible.

Jerks have a monopoly on these fun intense highs because Nice- guys are too mellow and calm. The human nervous system is attracted to intensity and cannot tell the difference between positive or negative intensity unless we give it the meaning ahead of time.

> *"There is no good or bad,*
> *just thinking that makes it so."*
> *-William Shakespeare*

Therefore, Jerks are able to be attractive and in many cases mentally and emotionally addictive to women. Sadly enough, with this addiction and a monopoly on its price, some Jerks charge the price of a physical abuse. I do not support this idea in any way. In a strange way, it is actually to a woman's benefit that I am teaching men to have the fun intense character traits of the wife beaters, because it will put the true wife beaters out of business by eliminating the monopoly they have. Women can then realize the emotional and mental highs that can be generated without the extraordinary price of a physical abuse.

Why do you think millions of children tell their parents they want to eat at McDonalds? Because they have such great food? No, it's because it is advertised as a great place to have fun while you eat and spend your money. Advertisers have known this for years, and spend hundreds of millions of dollars every year to get you to "link- up" good feelings to their products. Advertise yourself to women in a similar way by being the source of fun and good times. When women think of you, they should automatically link-up that you are out having a good time somewhere, and possibly with someone else. By doing fun, adventurous, spontaneous things consistently, women will consider you her "good time guy" or "mystery man on the side" because her current boyfriend wants to sit at home and watch television in his ratty T-shirt, and eat pizza. She will lie, cheat and steal in order to be with you to have a good time. She will buy into you through emotion and justify it with logic. Remember, it's been said that emotion is created by motion, so therefore, keep moving (like a Shark!) and find new and exciting places to go while you create fun intense highs for yourself and those lucky enough to be a member of your team.

With women addicted to you, it is about time to open your eyes to the greatest illusion and mystery in the Social Marketplace, which I call . . . .

# 12

## The Social Sales Pitch — Who's Selling Who?

*"Love: The delusion that one woman
differs from another."
-H.L. Mencken*

**WHO WOULD BE CRAZY** enough to pay an inflated premium price for a depreciating product that is selling at its all time high, and sold to you from a manipulative salesperson who wanted you to sign a contract stating that if you ever decided to default, it would cost you half of your assets and a garnishment of your income for years in the future? The answer is: the thousands of men that marry women every day!

What if I was even willing to tell you that the person selling the product knew ahead of time that it was highly addictive, and that the cost of goods sold (COGS for you accounting majors) was equal to zero, which translates to any price being pure profit - - Now how stupid do you think the buyer is?

Women are selling themselves with the same sales pitch that is used for cigarettes, alcohol and other drugs that have expensive prices, cheap highs, and a monopoly on an increasing price which is the result of addiction to the product. They use this sales pitch in order to get you emotionally involved with them, which eliminates any sense of logic your friends and family might try to pound into your head. It's true, in its natural form, the word illusion means: to deceive one's intellect. When are men at their most vulnerable point in their life and really feel they need someone to believe in them? The answer is between the ages of 20 to 30 as they are just starting a new career that they have been preparing for years. Wow! What a coincidence! That is exactly the same time frame that women are pitching their "product" in order to get what I call the "Ultimate Sale" - - Marriage!

*"Women are the Best*
*Salespeople in the World!*
*A Salesperson's Greatest Challenges,*
*Mental Satisfaction,*
*and Highest Emotional Highs*
*are Created from Making a Sale*
*to Those Who Were NEVER Interested*
*to Begin with.*
*This is Why the Customers*
*that Don't Look 'Hungry'*
*Will Always Be Fed."*
*-F.J. Shark*

You wouldn't be dumb enough to chase a used car salesperson and do business only when they had nothing better to do? So why would you even consider running after another salesperson trying to sell you her over-priced, depreciating product in the Social Marketplace? Her product probably already has too many miles put on it from all the other drivers who managed to blow her engine by "putting it to the test" and "seeing what that baby can do!" I'm not saying to only drive cars with no miles on them (i.e. virgins). Some products such as boats, airplanes and helicopters, are actually more valuable when they have a year or so of experience than when they were first built because it proves that they function properly. All I am suggesting is that she have her best times and most fun when she is with you, not through memories of somebody else.

If men get to buy into all that expensive, depreciating, addictive, legally binding good stuff - - NOT!, what are women getting in return? They are buying into men at their all time lowest point financially, with the security of a steady paycheck, which will add to the appreciation of his net-worth. So let's get this straight. Men buy into a physically attractive depreciating woman at their all time "beauty" high (24-28 years old) after they have had all their fun with Jerks and offered much lower prices for more, emotional, mental, and sexual service in the past. Woman buy into financially appreciating men at their all time financial low - - What a great deal! Where do I sign? - - NOT!

Smart women don't have to go to school and study incredibly boring subjects with hopes of getting out in the real world and finding a job. All they have to do is keep themselves physically attractive and wait for some Nice-guy to complete college and find a well paying career while she plays a game of cat and mouse with him by leading him around by the nose, making him believe he is chasing her, while she finds truth in the old female saying: "I'll let him chase me, till I catch him." Surprisingly enough, it usually is the guy that brings up the idea of marriage by this time, and women have all they can do to keep from laughing. The reason I say they are laughing is because it is equivalent to the customer selling himself on the product and closing himself on the deal without any effort on the part of the salesperson.

*"I do want to get rich,*
*but I never want to do*
*what there is to do to get rich."*
*-Gertrude Stein*

If there is one point you remember from this entire book, remember that in the Social Marketplace guys are not the sales people who should be focusing on selling the benefits they have to offer such as college or a career, but rather - - Women are the salespeople, and they are the best! Forget about impressing their parents with where you work and what your Father does for a living because they are the ones with their biological clocks ticking! They are the ones that need to find a buyer for their product and it is them against the clock. My grandfather told me years ago never to get married until I was at least 30 years old. At the time, I had no idea why he was telling me to wait for what I thought was an eternity. He already knew that the prices of women drop substantially around that age because women are more open and willing to give you a great deal on their product, the same way a used car salesperson is trying to unload this year's model because next year's new and improved models with a more sleek look and sexier appeal will be in the showroom soon. As long as women are trying to sell us their product, we might as well respond and act like the smartest investors and consumers in the world: 1) Shop around. Play the field. The only thing that truly keeps prices down is competition. Keeping an uncommitted relationship helps keep your costs down because women are lowering their prices as they try desperately to plant themselves in your mind. 2) Act like you are doing her the favor of going out with her the same way a shrewd businessman would treat the salesperson that is trying to sell him something expensive that he could buy from anybody else in the industry. Remember she is selling you on her product and you must gain her respect by saying "No!" to more of her ideas than you are saying "Yes" to. For example, how many days you are going to go out with her during the week? If you sell yourself like a drug, she will want 7 and you start the negotiating at 0, winding up with once or twice. 3) Complain about the level of "social" service and attention you are receiving from her by pointing out ways she can improve the relationship. She can literally spend a lifetime seeking your approval, improving the way she treats you and fulfilling every fantasy you have, as she keeps wondering if she is the one on your mind (every 8 seconds) and not that porn star or exotic dancer you keep talking about.

All of us have heard women say: "Even though he treats me like crap, I'm staying with him because I love him so much." What she is really saying is that she has invested so much into the relationship, the only way to get something back is to keep him interested and stick around in case he decides to do something sweet for her for a change, because there is no such thing as a "Love Collection Agency" in the Social Marketplace. She will stay in the relationship with hopes that someday he will

sign on the bottom line and the Ultimate Sale will be a done deal
- - Marriage!

### *"God is love,*
### *but get it in writing."*
### *-Gypsy Rose Lee*

Marriage had to be a woman's idea because what guy in his right mind would come up with the idea of not having sex with any other woman for the rest of his life and signing away at least 50% of his assets if something goes wrong. Someone once said: "Alimony is the system where by two people make a mistake, and one continues to pay for it." Let's see, a big chunk of my money leaves me every month, following the 50% of my assets, and 100% of her sex! Where do I sign? - - NOT!

If you are still considering marriage, at least get yourself a pre-nuptial agreement. The Marriage license is her legally binding "insurance policy" contract that guarantees she is taken care of in the event of a crisis within the Marriage. Where is your legally binding insurance policy? What kind of business person would be stupid enough to hold himself wide open to be taken advantage of by someone who could turn into his worst enemy? Her first response will be: "Pre-nups are not very romantic!" and you come back with: "Yeah! I agree - - and neither is Divorce!" If you decide on a wedding, I hope you stick her Father with the bill because an average wedding costs around $15,000.00 in cold hard American dollars! Wait! It gets better! (It can't get much worse! (I sound like a woman going out with a Jerk.)) The average cost of a one week honeymoon is over $3,500 - - Have a nice day!

I have come to the conclusion that dating and Marriage over the long term are more expensive than prostitution! I am not speaking from experience with a prostitute, nor do I encourage the idea. However, financially speaking, prostitution is cheaper and a much greater deal all the way around. Just for kicks, let's see how much sex would cost you through a 10 year Marriage and divorce as compared to prostitution, using my own statistics and beliefs: Average # of times a couple has sex over a 10 year period: 2 times per week x 52 weeks per year x 10 yrs. = 1,040 sexual encounters. She divorces you and receives 50 % of your accumulated assets from:

10 years of hard work. $150,000/2 = **$75,000+** 30-50% of all future earnings for the next 3-5 years. $35,000 x 4 yrs. x 40% = **$56,000+** All stupid vacations she planned for the both of you. $2,000 per vacation x 3 times per year x 10 yrs. = **$60,000+** If she doesn't work, then you are her meal ticket, $1,000 per month (her half) x 12 mo. x 10 yrs. = **$120,000+** her shelter provider ( including utilities), $450 per mo. (her half) x 12 mo. x 10 yrs. = **$54,000+** her 2 cars over a 10 year period, $15,000 x 2 = **$30,000+** total insurance coverage , $2,000 per year x 10 yrs. = **$20,000+** Miscellaneous crap she bought. $2,500 per year x 10 years = **$25,000**

We are not calculating clothing expenses because she better be naked and as ready and willing as a prostitute because **She financially cost you a total of $440,000**

**$440,000/1,040 sexual encounters = $423 per sexual encounter! (I hope you got your money's worth!!!)**

I understand that not all women sit around all day. They work! They have careers! I am woman, hear me roar! I totally support the E.R.A. in every way because: 1) Women have the most undervalued assets in the world. 2) It's about time they learn the value of money. 3) They can pay for the dates and begin to take us out for a  change!

They have come a long way (baby), and we shouldn't put them down for their efforts. After all, according to recent to recent surveys and general statistics, from

365 Meditations, Reflections & Restoratives for Women Who Do Too Much, by: Anne Wilson Schaef and 365 Days of Women 1994 Calendar, women today are: 5 times more likely than her mother to be a doctor, 15 times more likely to be a lawyer, 25 times more likely to be a dentist, and 30 times more likely to be an engineer. It's been said that women already control over 80% of the money in the entire world. They own 40% of the agricultural land America today. Women own 30% of all American businesses, and by the year 2,000 they are expected to own 50%!!! Today these women-owned firms employ more people than ALL of the Fortune 500 companies combined!!!

*"I've been called a tramp,*
*a harlot and a slut.*
*But in reality*
*I just act out the notion that a girl*
*can have fun and be sexual*
*at the same time . . . I may dress*
*like the traditional bimbo,*
*but I'm in charge.*
*And isn't that what feminism is all about?"*
*-Madonna*

In case you didn't already know, the word "Bitch" stands for: Being In Total Control of Him. We need women in control of more things, so they learn to take on responsibility and be more willing to handle it in the Social Marketplace. This will give us more of a chance to do more socializing and have more fun while they steer the relationship! "I am personally looking forward to the day when women will control the world and men can just focus on providing women with sex and emotional support at home after we finish watching our favorite football games." Solving the greatest mystery in the Social Marketplace will cause you to adopt . . . .

# 13

## The Identity and Character Traits of JERKS

*"We are what we think.
All that we are
arises with our thoughts.
With our thoughts,
we make our world."
-The Buddha*

**IN NATURE,** there are 3 categories of honey bees: 1) The workers, who gather food, take care of the young, and build a shelter providing security, 2) The Queen who lays eggs and does absolutely no work around the home, and 3) drones whose only real function is to fertilize the eggs of the Queen.

In the Social Marketplace, the Nice-guys play the role of the worker who becomes the source of security, while his wife (the Queen), is busy screwing around with guys who are primarily interested in just having fun (drones). I understand that not every woman cheats on her man or has sex with multiple partners. However, you should be aware of the findings of a recent study that calculated the number of condoms purchased by American women EVERYDAY - - 220,000+ !!! Remember, that's just the women in America who choose to have safe sex, and not mentioning the inventory supply of condoms they have in their purses or that men buy. My point is that if you are not getting your fair share of the sexual pie, realize that somebody else is, and most women cut out their own piece of the pie first and have fun with or without you.

So what role do you want to play in nature? Just think, if the bees had their own encyclopedia collection on humans the way we do on them - - Do you want to be known as the sucker who pays all the dues, does all the work in the relationship, and receives no membership with the queen? I have an even scarier question for you: What identity do you think you have in a relationship?

### *"Man is what he believes."*
### *-Anton Checkhov*

Somebody once said: "All the world's a stage." If so, what character are you? Regardless of your answer, a better question is: "What character do you want to be? You have the opportunity to play the leading role on the stage in your life which will return to you the pay and benefits a leading role commands.

Would you rather have the highest batting average in triple "A" baseball, or the lowest average in the major leagues? The correct answer is the lowest average in the major leagues because you are still considered to be in the major leagues. If the player with the highest batting average in the farm team was really so hot, he would have been playing in the majors yesterday.

I remember listening to a major league baseball player as a guest speaker. He said that at one time, he felt he was in a batting slump and had a depressing .252 average. One day an all-star .340 hitter asked him some personal questions to see if he could help him. One of the questions the .340 hitter asked was: "What percentage hitter do you think you are?". The .252 hitter said: "About a .250 hitter." The .340 hitter said: "Exactly! That's why you get the results of a .250 hitter! I believe I am a .340 hitter and therefor, I get the breaks of a .340 hitter!"

### "Things do not change; we change."
### -Henry David Thoreau

If you want to change your batting average in the Social Marketplace, you must start with your own thoughts and actions. Matching the thoughts and actions of the most socially sexcessful people is the only way to get the results of the most socially sexcessful people.

### "We are what we repeatedly do."
### -Aristotle

When I first started as a registered representative in the financial advisor/stock broker industry I was 22 years old, and fresh out of college. Who in their right mind would hand over their hard earned money to a young, inexperienced stranger in another state over the phone? The first thing I learned is that you have to at least give people the impression that you are not new to the industry or they will not trust you. In other words, you have to first believe in yourself and your product and then other people will as well.

*"If you think you can,*
*or think you can't,*
*you're right."*
*-Henry Ford*

The next step is to make it appear that you are not hungry for the sale. Nice-guys are hungry for women, as a result don't have any women, and as a result get more hungry for women. They fall victim to this downward spiral until it has picked up so much momentum that they are spinning out of control.

The social truth is that women do not want to have sex with a guy if he is a virgin because he will not be confident in what he is doing which is a result of not having any experience on the topic. I believe the other reason is that most women feel they have a Mercedes of a body and performance when it comes to sex. They figure if anybody's first car is a Mercedes, they won't appreciate it, and the driver will assume that all the cars (women) in the industry (Social Marketplace) have the same type of quality. Therefore, their conclusion is to only have sex with guys who have someone to compare them to. This way she can clearly see that if he comes back for more, he is preferring her sex over some other woman's that he had notched in his belt and scraped as a slash on the headboard of his bed. She doesn't trust Mr. Virginity because she knows even if he stays with her for the rest of his life, he will always wonder what another flavor tasted like.

I'm sure you have heard the story about Roger Banister who was the first human to ever run a 4 minute mile. Within one month of him breaking the 4 minute mile, over thirty people broke it as well. Within one year over 300 people accomplished it. Sometimes we are our own worst enemy because we actually believe the limiting beliefs that we set up for ourselves. We tend to underestimate the 3 pound piece of biological matter (our brain) that controls our heart to beat 100,000 times a day and pump 6,00 quarts of blood through 60,000 miles of blood vessels. This is not a crash course in Biology 101. It has been said, however, that your mind will give you the reality of your conscious thoughts. In English, this translates to the old phrase: "Where the mind goes, the body will follow." Did you ever notice that people are like a self-leveling piece of clay as they usually fill in the holes to whatever role is needed to be played in a relationship? Who ever can hold their breath longer and not take on any of the responsibilities is usually the person who has control, grants approval to the other and benefits big time within the relationship.

> *"Who ever loves the least*
> *controls the relationship."*
> *-Unknown*

If you signed up for and tried out for the role of the nice-guy and are now complaining because you are receiving nice-guy pay - - Shut up! Who told you to pick the nice-guy costume? The secret to remember is that YOU have first choice of what costume and role you want to play in the relationship. Women will fill in the holes with whatever is left over, because they want you to be happy.

> *"The woman will please first,*
> *whom ever the man does."*
> *-F.J. Shark*

This means if the man puts a smile on his face pleasing himself first, then the woman will please him first as well. However, in the case of a Nice-guy, he puts the smile on her face and pleases her first, and as a result she pleases herself first as well. Women are willing to take care of you in every way and play the role of a nurse providing you are a patient. Why would a nurse try to help and heal a person that was healthy and in better shape than she is? This will add to her feeling needed by you, and build incredible support in the relationship. You are too busy having a good time, so therefore she has to assume the responsibility or the relationship will die (like the patient). If you happen to find a women interested in you that is acting more wild than you are, the only way to get her to show the least bit of responsibility for the relationship, is to remember my Theory of the Crazyman which states: "The only thing a crazyman fears is a crazier man!". Therefore, you have to be even more wild and crazy than she is in order to get her to respond to you and make her realize that she has met her match as she begins to take responsibility for the relationship because: 1) you won't, and 2) she is addicted to you and wants to make sure that you stay with her to create more new intense fun highs. This type of adventurous, spontaneous, playful fun is what makes you so damn addictive.

### "The great man is he that does not lose his child's heart." -Mencius

Rock'n Roll musicians not only are living out their dreams and passions, but they are like playful little children on vacation away from the responsibilities and homework of school. Most of them even have an identity with a tilt toward dangerous - - which is a girl magnet.

*"Women like to sit down with trouble
as if it were knitting."
-Ellen Glasgow*

I remember when I saw the backstage interview with a selected group of fans with one of the most notorious bands in the world. The band was famous for coming to a city and helping to rearrange the furniture and decorations of the hotel they were staying at. Not all the hotels wanted this new image, so the band was banned from many of the hotels in many cities. A reporter asked one of the hot female fans if she realized just how dangerous the band was, and she said, "I know, that's exactly why my friends and I are here." Yes, another thrill seeker who will laugh in the face of danger and snicker in the face of death, all for the almighty sense of having a good time and fun intense memories to tell to their grandchildren.

For all the "piggish" and perverted traits that women claim that men have, I find it utterly amazing that the qualities that are an attraction and focal point in the area of dating, such as: mysterious and teasing (not knowing if he is going to call her or where she stands in a relationship), adventurous, spontaneous, unpredictable, even the ability to get mad with hot-tempered emotion, all sound exactly like they can be found in what she wants in the area of sex. A woman believes that if you represent these qualities and character traits in the dating arena, then they will also be found in the sexual department as well. If she is lucky enough to find a guy that has all of these, then she knows she is in for one hell of an encounter that will put the "X" in "Peak Sexual Experience". This is the type of guy that women would die for and leave the alter for if they are standing up there waiting to marry some other guy. We all know women that would leave the relationship they are in currently at three o'clock in the morning, if the other mystery man called her.

One time a girl asked me to give her a wake-up call at 6:45 in the morning because I would already be up and she needed to go to an important business meeting. A true Jerk would not have remembered to call at all, but I knew it was really important to her to get up on time. I, on the other hand, did not want to be known as Mr. Dependable. I thought about how I could tick her off and still get the job done. At 6:35 I woke her up out of deep R.E.M. sleep, and in a loud outrageous voice yelled, "This is the snooze button! You've got 10 minutes to wake up!" and hung up the phone. Do you think she remembered it as a funny moment? Do you think she will talk about it with her friends because it was unique? Will her friends wonder if I am that outrageous or will they ask me out and see for themselves? The bottom line is, she got up in time. I was unpredictable and outrageous, and I got her friends asking me out. What a deal!

When you have the jerk identity and character traits, you'll start . . . .

# 14

## Making Yourself a CHALLENGE!

*"Reason guides but a small part of man,
and that's the least interesting.
The rest obeys feeling,
true or false, and passion, good or bad."*
*-Joseph Rue*

**WHAT IS** the opposite of love? If you said - hate, you are wrong, and thank God you own this book! The opposite of love is disinterest. Therefore, if you have strong interest in something which takes up time and space in your day and mind, it is a fair statement to make that you love the idea. These ideas could be as strong as your career or as relaxing as a hobby, - truly something that gets you up early and keeps you up late. Something that you would do even if people didn't pay you for it. Regardless if it is preparing income taxes, selling stock, playing the guitar or playing the violin, it is considered to be one of your passions.

If your passions come first, second and third in your life,

women will literally spend a lifetime trying to get you to transfer those strong, emotional, committed feelings you show for your passions over to her. By transferring those feelings over to her, you will be stuffed and mounted, and she will spend her time hunting down another guy who is not such an easy kill.

Remember that girl in school that you had a crush on, but she liked someone else who didn't even know that she was alive? The other guy was skinny, ugly and financially poor - - So how was he getting so much attention from the girl? The same way rock'n roll musicians in your local bar do it - - they have a PASSION! A passion for music, the band itself, playing an instrument, and the dream of making it to the big time someday. It shows the girls that the guy is capable of creating his own fun. He is on stage doing wild, crazy, outrageous, spontaneous and unpredictable things. (Sounds like one hell of a sexual encounter to her!)

*"A musician must make music,*
*an artist must paint,*
*a poet must write,*
*if he is to be ultimately*
*at peace with himself."*
*-Abraham Maslow*

Remember that time some girl that you didn't even care about was interested in you? Maybe you didn't even know she existed. You were completely interested and excited about something else that you had going on in your life, and this girl was practically worshipping the ground you walked on. How powerful and influential were you in the relationship? That level of respect and priority can be attained in any relationship if you just E.A.T. (get Excited About other Things). I'll never forget the meaning behind the speech of the selected Senior at my Freshman orientation in high school. He started off by saying that our high school offered him the opportunity to create many memorable moments because of it's wide variety of sports and outside activity programs. By mentioning that we will never remember the grade we received on a geometry or history test, it was clear that he wanted us to adopt a simple idea - - DON'T be an 8 A.M. to 3 P.M. student! This secret message is what made your four years some of the best years of your life or a bliss that you try not to bring up in conversation.

I believe women have a strong need to over-rule and over-ride another woman or idea that captures the interest of your mind. I have seen women convince guys to sell their Corvette and motorcycle (the very thing that created the spark of her interest in him in the first place) in order to make his mind scramble for a new #1 passion in his life, and the obvious choice would be her. If he does get rid of his passion, it will also make him less interesting and socially exciting to other women. Therefore, on the simple move of convincing him to forget about his passion, she is killing two birds with one stone: 1) she becomes his passion, 2) eliminates the attraction from her competition - - any other woman!

If you are underestimating the power behind this then realize that there are some women that I know of personally that go after priests! For years people in our parish could not understand why this was occurring. The woman did not just try to go after one priest, she went after several! The hidden motive behind her sinful actions was trying to get a man to transfer the love and commitment, that he had for God over to her. This would reward her with the incredible ego boost in her mind that she was more influential and powerful than God Himself! Wow! I think it's going to take more than a few "Hail Mary's" to get her out of that one! As long as we are on the topic, what was the one tree in the Garden of Eden that Eve wound up eating from? - - The one she was told she couldn't have! Of course, she could not assume responsibility for her actions. If she couldn't blame it on Adam, she found a way to pull him down with her as she worked out a deal with the serpent to sucker Adam and the rest of us to get thrown out of the utopian garden forever. (See, even guys that wrote the Bible thousands of years ago knew how manipulative women are!) You have to become the "forbidden fruit" that she desires because she cannot have it. If you show her that you are 'not hungry' for sex, and not interested in her as a girlfriend, then she will want nothing more than to prove you wrong and sell you on the idea of herself by using all her sales techniques and womanly persuasion to lie, cheat and steal in order to get you interested in her. If you prove to her that you don't have time for her, then there will be nothing more important to her except distracting you and pulling you away from what you are focused on, even if it takes her a lifetime to do it.

On a more down to earth level (no pun intended), there was a girl I knew in college that had been going out with a guy for over two years. I asked her how it all started, and she said that they met through one of his friends. I thought that he set them up, but the truth was that she was really after his friend to begin with. I then asked her why she was faithfully going out with her boyfriend, who was the 2nd choice. She said that in the beginning it was just to make the other guy jealous, but then her boyfriend cheated on her and had her emotionally tied to him from that point. I said, "So therefore, when he made it clear to you that you were really no big deal to him, you had to sell yourself to him in a more meaningful way because he was interested in other women and not such an easy kill, right?" She said: "Yeah all that is true. He was quite a challenge because he was never really interested in me to begin with and I still have to remind him about me to this day." I asked her if she had plans to marry him and she said: "Oh definitely! Someday that will be my way of having more of his mind on me."

This girl will spend her life trying to capture more of her boyfriend's attention and own a greater piece of his mind. Do you think the relationship would have lasted more than a week or two if he did not cheat on her or find some other way of proving to her that she didn't come first in his life? By now she would have forgotten his name, as she'd be busy chasing after some other guy that she cannot have. Isn't it strange the way everybody wants to join the club that won't let them in, or buy the car that they can't afford?

When I was in 5th grade, I organized my first garage sale. A foreign woman was interested in buying one of my grandmother's new handkerchief sets that were donated to me and still in the original package. She began trying to talk me down from $1.00 to $.50 (yes, 50 pennies!). I said: "No! It's only a dollar." With my verbal response, the woman next to her said: "Well I'll buy it for a dollar!" The foreign woman quickly grabs the box away from the lady and begins screaming: "Mine! Mine!", as she hands me $2.00 (so I wouldn't start an auction to the highest bidder) and runs off. The meaning behind the story is when you are selling your product (you), in the Social Marketplace, and there is only one girl currently interested in you, don't be surprised if she tries to negotiate a lower price (doing less for you as you do more for her) because there are no other interested buyers. Putting yourself on the upward social spiral includes having fun relationships with several women so that you can sell yourself to the highest bidder and pay out the least amount because of the competition among the women.

You may have already come to your own conclusion, and believe that your only real challenge with women is sex. On the other hand, considering that a woman already knows she can have sex with whom ever she wants to, where she wants to, when ever she wants to, then her only real challenge is to: 1) get you, and 2) keep you interested as a boyfriend/husband. if you are an easy kill, don't even worry about #2 because you will never make it that far! If you make it to #2 and do not have a roving eye open for something better, then she will!

Remember that one Christmas that you wanted some cool new toy so bad that it was all you could think about? You probably didn't even get any sleep on Christmas Eve, as you wondered all night if that toy was really under the tree, waiting to be opened in the morning. If the toy would have been just handed to you exactly when you had the intention of desiring it, the excitement and thrill of anticipation and "not knowing" are over. The same idea holds true for strippers. If they were to come right on stage completely naked, the dirty thoughts of you wondering what is under their clothes would never exist (What a crime!). The bikini or lingerie that reveals a lot, but not enough, is what stirs up your curiosity and makes your imagination run wild. This is comparable to not putting all of your cards on the table by telling her everything about your life in the smallest detail.

## "He knows little, who tells his wife all he knows." -Thomas Fuller

Leave some room for mystery and make her wonder where you are and what you are doing. Your passions should be the busy "push away" that takes you right to the top of her list of what she wants because she knows that she can't have you.

The thrill of the hunt will keep her coming back for more. There was a poem entitled; "The Hunt" or 'The Great hunt" I don't remember the author's name, but I'll never forget the story. it described two friends that talked all year long about their annual event of hunting a specifically marked deer in the woods. Some years they would not even spot the deer and other years they couldn't get close enough to shoot it. The next year, one of the hunters met and cornered the deer unexpectedly. The deer froze stiff in fear of being killed. The hunter raised his gun, lined up the deer in his scope, and . . . put the gun back down as the deer ran to its freedom. His buddy could not believe that they had talked about this for years and now that they were able to accomplish it, he refused to pull the trigger. The hunter who let the deer get away, explained his actions by saying, "If I killed it, what would we talk about and do next year?"

While working on your passions and making yourself a challenge, you need to be employing . . . .

# 15

## The 10 Commandments of JERKS

*"The best soldier does not attack.*
*The superior fighter succeeds without violence.*
*The greatest conqueror*
*wins without a struggle."*
*-Lao-Tsu, Tao Teh King*

**DO YOU REMEMBER** that stuffed animal that was your best friend for many years? It probably had food stains on it along with a missing eye. But, damn it! It was yours and regardless if people made fun of it, or tried to replace it with a similar one, it just wasn't the same.

Every year for seven years, my mother would bring home a new Harris bank lion doll named "Hubert", and most of them are still in the original plastic wrapping to this day. I guess I didn't feel like breaking in any others after the first one or two. I wouldn't believe it, but the first few stuffed lions were at one point in time just as stiff as #7 that remains in its plastic wrapping. The first one got the most use because it was obviously around the longest and survived much wear and tear from my imaginative playing. I would flip him into the air as if we were some strange circus act and then drag him behind me for countless miles within the house. If someone were to have given me a stuffed lion that was already broken in and had some other persons' spit and dried food on it, I would have thrown it away immediately.

Therefore, in the Social Marketplace, what makes you think that some girl is going to stay in a relationship with you if you were "broken in" by some other girl! I'm not talking about sex. I'm talking about a girl having to invest her own time, effort and energy into you and the relationship so that she has a self-interest in staying even when times get ugly. If she hasn't, she will quickly get bored with you because she has nothing to change about you, and has no actual loss on her part because she did not have any of her own love and emotion invested in you. One of the main reasons why women stay with wife beaters and abusive alcoholics is because they feel that they can change him and keep throwing good emotion and love after bad. She feels like the captain who has so much invested in his ship (relation-ship) that he decides to go down with it when it sinks.

Arguments, problems and upsets are an active part of every healthy relationship. If two people agree on everything, why are there two of you when only one is required? Therefore, in order to be REAL and not a "Too good to be true" person, you must reveal your faults and differences within the relationship. One girl actually said to me: "Don't be afraid to mess up sometimes. In fact, I will probably love you more because I will know the real you!" So actually you are doing her a favor by acting irrespon-sible, selfish and egotistical because that is the only way the relationship will go from being a seed in the dirt to a blossoming flower in the garden of the Social Marketplace. (Gee, Shark, you're so romantic!), or a high risk penny stock that now has the ability to trade on a more developed exchange with the rest of the blue-chip stocks.

All of this starts with you being irresponsible enough in the beginning so that she has to put on the "emotional nurse" costume and assume the responsibility of taking care of the relationship so it doesn't die. Don't be afraid to forget key anniversary dates, names of her family members, and her family's birthdays, because it shows that you have other things on your mind and she needs to do a better job of selling herself to you. By now her family members are criticizing her for staying with you. This is the greatest place to be because now you are the product she has to sell to them as she has the opportunity to prove them wrong and actually look for things that are good and decent about you, or make them up, (which she probably already has). As a basic guideline, I have created the :

## The 10 Commandments of JERKS

### 1) Thou shalt NEVER worry about the competition, because thy competition does not worry about thy!

If you think a girl has a boyfriend or she claims to be "seeing someone", don't even flinch and say: "Yeah, so what's your point? I go out with other people for fun too." This will let her know that you really don't need her because you are not hungry and therefore, gives her the chance to sell herself to you - - the uninterested buyer - - for a much cheaper price than the last hungry guy that went out with her.

## 2) Thou shalt not return all thy phone calls!

You're busy! Remember? You are not waiting home for the phone to ring, you are a Diamond Player who is out having a good time, maybe even meeting a more beautiful girl! (Well at least that's what the girl who called will be thinking!)

## 3) Thou shalt cancel-out on the dates of your choice with or without warning or previous notice!

If you cancel a date or don't even show up, she will spend the evening thinking about you even if she decides to go out with another guy. She will wonder if she did something wrong or if you still want to go out with her at all. In any case, she will want you even more and realizes that she has to do an even better job of selling herself to you in order to make an even greater impact on your mind so that you will think of her more often and remember her the next time. She figures if she made a lasting impression on you, then you would be here right now. But you're not!

## 4) Thou shalt tell at least one lie to a woman!

The one lie Jerks always tell women is that they have been with some other girl who was much better in any area, especially physically and sexually. The question usually comes up from the girl after an intimate moment, when she knows the time is right, and asks, "Shark, have you ever been with some other girl who is better than me physically or sexually?" (With specific body parts and positions mentioned and not used here in this example!) If you have ever been asked a similar question and respond with "No" (meaning she is the best thing you have ever seen and been with in any way), you my friend are stuffed, mounted and forgotten about! Even if she stays in the relationship, she now realizes that no other girl has offered as much love and/or sex, so why should she? Immediately the price goes up as you wind up giving more and receiving less. You are now back to being in supply instead of in demand - - GAME OVER !!! Do not pass go. Do not collect $200.

## 5) Thou shalt be late and never wait!

I do not like being predictable, yet I need to be exact about things like time. So therefore, instead of having women set their clocks by me when I say that I will pick them up at 9:00, I am there exactly at 12 minutes or so after the time I stated. I know ahead of time when I will exactly arrive, yet I remain unpredictable to her because it shows I was busy doing something else. As far as you waiting for ANYTHING - - Don't! If you get put on hold or call waiting for longer than 10 seconds - - Hang up! She had enough time to tell the other person to call back. Your time is valuable to you and she has to realize that as well. In the area of sex, compare a woman to a bank and sex/love to money. Who do banks loan money to? The answer is: to people who can prove they don't need the money to begin with! Every millionaire and billionaire in the world can get a loan because banks realize that they can afford to pay it back and it is no big deal. If you are not getting enough money out of your bank then leave! Banks are in business to loan you money providing you can show them you don't need it to begin with. If all you want is good conversation, then call a 900 number, don't have a girlfriend!

> **"Money, it turned out**
> **was exactly like sex,**
> **you thought of nothing else**
> **if you didn't have it**
> **and thought of other things**
> **if you did. "**
> **-James Baldwin**

*6) Thou shalt borrow money*
*(The real stuff with the Presidents on it!)*
*from at least 5 women this month!*

See how long it takes them to ask for it back, or how good they want to get to know you because you owe them something.

*7) Thou shalt have dirty magazines scattered around*
*your living area and posters of as many half naked*
*(or naked) women on your walls as you can find room*
*for!*

This will show her that you at least know that hotter babes are somewhere on the planet, and she will do everything she can in her power to get and keep them off your mind.

## 8) Thou shalt be a regular at exotic dancing gentlemen's clubs!

(It sounds so much better than the words "strip bar" doesn't it?) Let her know the exotic dancers know you by name and that some of them have secret pet names for you as well. Be sure you can rattle off all of the dancers' names in one breath, it will show you were paying attention.

## 9) Thou shalt idolize a woman or two that you probably will never meet!

Take an interest in one or two professional models, movie actresses, female rock'n roll stars or porno queens. (You might have to watch the movies a couple hundred times just so you can be sure to pick your favorites!

## 10) Thou shalt not bring up the idea of future dates!

Don't bring up weddings, concerts, birthdays, etc. that are not occurring this month. If you do, she will be under the assumption that not only will she still be in your life at that time, but she will be your date to the event. Keep her wondering, be mysterious. In other words, know when to SHUT-UP!

If any of these commandments get you into hot water for an uncomfortable amount of time, you might have to say the "S" word - - Sorry! Use it sparingly, and, if possible, do not use it at all. Just keep in mind that:

## *"It's always easier to ask forgiveness than permission."*
### *-Unknown*

These 10 Jerk Commandments can enable you to be . . . .

# 16

## The Gift that Keeps on Giving — NOT!

*"If you like to be sweet
and give a lot in a relationship,
then give a little,
so you are around long enough
to give a lot!"*
*-F.J. Shark*

*I COULDN'T WAIT* to see her face. After weeks of searching, my family and I finally found what I wanted to hunt down. It was a little stuffed bear with a perfume bottle which had been the class Christmas wish of the girl whose name I had drawn for the "Secret Santa" party in grammar school. Now that the hunt was complete, I figured she would really like me, and probably figured she owed me her first born, simply by the way she had been talking about the bear to her friends.

When the day came to exchange gifts, I didn't even remember what I asked for from my "Secret Santa" because I was so focused on making this one girl happy. She unwrapped the gift without any enthusiasm or excitement at all. A loud noise was caused by my jaw hitting the ground as she made it clear to me that this really wasn't the actual bear she wanted. The room got even colder when she asked me on the spot if she could swap it for her friend's brush set gift that she received from her "Secret Santa". I was speechless. The shock of the moment echoed in my mind for years to come.

The disappointment of giving all you can in a relationship, and having your heart smashed into a million pieces right before your eyes, as you see all your effort shrivel up and blow away, has caused people to fear even the thought of giving. The logical solution is not to give or invest any emotion at all, and therefore have nothing to lose. People avoid the stock market for the same reason. What people have figured out in the stock market and have yet to figure out in the Social Marketplace is that you should only be willing to invest what you can afford to lose. Investing all your emotional, mental and physical ability into a single relationship is just as stupid as investing your life savings into a high risk stock.

If you won every time you played a slot machine, the fun would evaporate because you would eventually become bored, lose interest and move on to another game or casino. When you have the opportunity to give in a relationship, think of yourself as a Las Vegas slot machine. If you reward people every time and become so predictable with your giving that others expect it of you, don't be surprised if they move on to another person, (slot machine), that is more of a challenge, unpredictable and fun. Remember, if gambling rewarded you every time you played, "Gambler's Anonymous" would not exist, because nobody would be addicted to it.

The truth is, to this day, I still like to be a giver in my

relationships. Many of you probably like to be a giver as well, and as a result were burned for your efforts. I saw the need for basic guidelines to follow when you are giving to women in relationships. I call them:

## Shark's Rules for Giving

**1)** Allow people to enjoy the gift of giving to you for a change! This stops you from playing the role of the martyr and be on the receiving end of the stick.

**2)** Keep in mind the Minimum/Maximum Theory in the Social Marketplace which states: "Giving the maximum gets you the minimum and giving the minimum gets you the maximum." A scientific research study was completed on the life span of rats comparable to their food in-take. By cutting the food supply of the one group of rats in half, they were able to double their life span. Therefore, a popular saying in the health field toward people who like to eat which states: "If you like to eat a lot, then eat a little, so that you are here long enough to eat a lot." Apply this inversely proportional idea to giving in relationships so that you are not dumped because you flooded the engine and didn't even have a chance to drive. "If you like to give in relationships, then give a little, so that you are around long enough to give a lot!"

**3)** Give on an infrequent, unpredictable basis so that nobody EXPECTS it from you. If you give too often it will go unrecognized and unappreciated because you have fallen into the trap of being routine. Avoiding this trap includes being spontaneous, adventurous and unpredictable, which will cause great emotional highs in both you and the girl you are interested in getting addicted to you.

**4)** Give only to people that not only strongly need what you have to offer, but more importantly APPRE-CIATE WHATEVER EFFORT you put in and recognize that you really went out of your way. If you are with some girl that does not appreciate you - - DUMP HER! Quit throwing good time, effort and energy after bad. The fact is that there are about 2,500,000,000 (2.5 Billion) women on this planet and most of them will never even have the opportunity to meet you personally. Therefore, if you are not receiving the level of appreciation that you think you deserve from the girl you are with, it is your own fault.

Considering that over 12 million American children live in poverty, 100,000 are homeless, and 27 die every day as a result, you have plenty of appreciative people who could use your act of giving even if the Social Marketplace rejects what you have to offer. The charity idea of "Toys for Tots" is something that wild, black leather wearing, motorcycle riding gentleman take part in and demonstrates to the women in their lives that: "There really is a "Golden Heart" under all that wickedness."

A few Thanksgivings ago I convinced my family to donate the free turkey that we received from the store as a result of saving up special coupons. After calling a couple of churches to donate the turkey, I found out that specific organizations within the church had their own plans and did not even want my donation because they already had enough for the less fortunate people they were helping. The average person would have stopped there and got mad at the churches that rejected the gift - - NOT ME! I got mad and did something about it! I got so mad that I called up another church and offered to help a family on my own. I figure somebody needed help somewhere. Sister Mary, who did not know me from Adam, answered the phone and heard the sincerity in my convincing voice and offered me the name of a less fortunate family in her parish that she thought could really benefit from my donation. I called up the family and told them who I was, who referred me to them and that I would like to help them. The man on the other end of the phone seemed extremely grateful and appreciative. He then said something that I will never forget: "Even if you have any extra clothing or left over food, we could use it." I thought to myself, "How desperate do you have to be in order to ask a complete stranger over the phone for clothes and food for you and your children?" It was obvious that the man and his family needed more than just my turkey. I decided to do more than just dropping off a turkey. I arranged it with the man and Sister Mary to dress up like Santa Clause to celebrate Christmas with the man,his wife and their four children.

With some help, I bought them all special gifts that they specifically wanted as well as food they really needed and couldn't afford otherwise. When I arrived at their sad looking apartment building, I noticed that they all lived in only 1 room with a mattress up against the wall for the entire family to sleep on at night. The children really believed that I was Santa Claus as they opened their gifts with great excitement. The one boy didn't want me to leave because we were having so much fun crawling around on the floor playing with his new trucks. As I left, I thought about what led me all the way to this moment from wanting to deliver a turkey. If you feel that you get burned for your efforts of giving, you might be right. However, you probably have been giving to the people who already possess what you have to offer.

Since that time I have created the F.J. SHARK Foundation which helps less fortunate people from various walks of life. Its future events include; Blood drives, food drives, clothing drives, walk-a- thons, dance-a-thons and much more that will benefit people directly, as well as involvement with other non-profit organizations from the Red Cross to the Salvation Army.

Now that you have the art of giving and all of these other Jerk strategies mastered, you will soon find out . . . .

# 17

## Where this Book Really Begins

*"Somebody should tell us,*
*right at the start of our lives,*
*that we are dying.*
*Then we might live life to the limit,*
*every minute of every day.*
*Do it! I say.*
*Whatever you want to do, do it now!*
*There are only so many tomorrows."*
*-Michael Landon*

**EVER HEAR** the story about the man in Lousiana who was waiting for a flood to strike the town? It began to rain, and before long, the depth of the water reached the stairs of the man's house. A rescue boat comes along trying to save the man and the man says, "No! God will save me!!" The boat goes away and time passes. The water is now higher and the man is standing on tables as the second boat pulls up and the man says, "No! Go away! God will save me!" The second boat goes away and time passes. By now the water is so high that the man has to sit up on the roof of his house. A helicopter flies over head and lowers a ladder to the man. The man says, "No! Get outa here! God will save me!" The helicopter flies away, the water rises, and the man drowns. He goes to heaven and tells God that he is a bit peeved at the fact that his faith and prayers were not rewarded. God then says, "What more did you want me to do ?!? I sent 2 boats and a helicopter!"

It's too late for the man from Louisiana to realize and use the help that he was offered, but it isn't too late for you. How ever you heard about this book, you not only found it through the mysterious forces of the universe, but you invested your money and time into it. In any event, I appreciate the opportunity to have such a powerful impact on your mind and I'm sure you will never forget reading this book. The fun emotional highs that you create will last you a lifetime of memories.

Use the social "inside information" in this book as a wake-up call to have the Social Marketplace work in your favor. Take your life to the level of the Diamond Player, .340 hitter, and spontaneous, adventurous little child. Think with your brain and not any other part of your body. Sell yourself like a drug, make adjustments to have situations benefit yourself for a change, and remember - - don't fall asleep behind the wheel in the car of your life. You are a Lamborghini, and they don't have financing!

Create some memories in the Social Marketplace that you will never forget. If you don't think it's possible to be that memorable, just ask the stars in the sky. Next time it is a clear night, go outside and look up at the stars, which are all nothing more than memories. Each star burned out millions of years ago, and what you are seeing is the remainder of the light traveling 186, 282 miles per second in our direction. The beams of light that are reaching you at this moment, took millions of years to arrive here. So as soon as you take a picture of the stars in the sky, they are already millions of years old because if you wanted to see what the source of the light looks like right now at this moment, the only way to do it is to wait millions of years for it to get here.

Who ever came up with the phrase: "Don't worry be happy" was right. If you still feel the need to worry, then send $8 to a real business in Oakland California, where three people will worry for you. Seriously, it's been said that about 90% of what we worry about never comes true and 90% of what happens to us we don't worry about anyway. Bring out the irresponsible, adventurous, spontaneous child in you and find truth to the saying: "We do not stop playing because we grow old, we grow old because we stop playing." Nobody ever said on their death bed: "I wish I would have spent more time at the office!" So make your life extraordinary while you are still here.

Picture a Christmas Eve with an entire team of family and friends in their winter sweaters, decorating the tree by the fireplace as they listen to holiday songs and look out the window at the white gentle snow falling. The only problem is that you are not in the picture! You are on the outside looking in! How cheated do you feel knowing that others are having fun, creating memories to last them a lifetime, and you are outside in the process of getting frostbite?!

Regardless if you are a man or a woman, I believe that we all want and desire the same thing from relationships - - Memorable moments. We all want to have fun and exciting stories to tell our grandchildren, yet most people spend the majority of their time planning their life and forgetting about the moment they are in. These are the same people that come to the end of their life and say: "I wish I woulda, coulda, shoulda . . ." .

When I used to go camping with the scouts, some of us would stay up all night and play war games in the woods, raid other camps, and dodge M.P.'s which were there for security purposes. One time we even carried a sleeping scout from another troop out into the middle of the field where mass was going to be said the next morning. He woke up finding about three hundred people and a priest smiling at him as they sang the opening song to the mass. The scouts in our troop that fell asleep and got a good night's rest can NEVER bring those moments back because they are gone forever and the only thing remaining is a memory. Today, I bet they wished that their decision would have been to break more rules and get less sleep!

The choice is yours. You are the only person responsible for your own fun, so ask yourself: "What side of the Christmas window do you want to be on?" And most importantly, just remember the old phrase: "At the end of your life you will only have two types of relationship memories. The way it was, and the way it could have been! I don't expect you to carry this book around and look things up as you need them, so master it! Take the training wheels off and ride the wind, go off road, and blaze your own trail. You will be amazed about how many women follow you because you are having fun. Use the social magic of the other peoples' experiences that you learned about in this book, and learn from their mistakes and achievements.

One of my Passions is magic and studying the history of a man named Harry Houdini - - the greatest escape artist of all time. A popular story about Houdini, that I heard, took place around the time that he was becoming quite popular in the eyes of most Americans for his unique ability to escape from anything. A city challenged him to escape from their new and improved jail.

Houdini took on the challenge and worked relentlessly for hours to unlock the cell door. He became physically exhausted and was about to give up. To rest, he leaned on the cell door. And it opened! Because it had never been locked in the first place! I'm here to tell you up front that the doors of respect and priority that you were told and believed to be locked up and monopolized on by only a select few is the Emperor's new clothes! - - It's all a lie! The only place it can be locked is in your own mind. Only you determine which doors will open in the Social Marketplace through only accepting what you believe you deserve!

You have a simple choice about how women view and respond to you. You can either be the one who listens to their problems and bails them out of trouble after they were "up to no good"; or you can be the one they were being "up to no good" with!

So get out there and have some fun, because this is not where the book ends, but rather where it all begins.

Expect More

Accept Less!

-F.J. Shark

# Exclusive Interview:
## FJ Shark, "How To Be The Jerk Women Love"

## by Ross Jeffries

FJ Shark is one of those rare guys– a direct, to the point, on the ball straight shooter in a world full of clowns. He's the creator of the outrageous tape series, "How To Be The Jerk Women Love" and a guy after my own sleazy heart. I interviewed Shark in his palatial "Shark Tank" headquarters in Chicago.

Ross Jeffries: Shark, What is it that jerks do that seems to create this overwhelming desire in women to be with them?

FJ Shark: They create such an interest by not being interested at all. By never really accepting the women as their girlfriend, it takes the woman using all of her sales techniques, meaning her body, to sell him on the idea that he should be with her.

RJ: But what is it that jerks do initially to create that desire that women want to be around them?

FJS: They create a fun, intense high. And that is, they offer a sample of Themselves, just the way drugs are sold in this country. The reason why drugs are a hundred billion dollar industry here is not because they have such great salesmen, it's because they have a product that makes people feel good. So with a jerk, the first samples he gives a woman are free, just like drugs, and they can be almost like a free sample joint, if you will, and then the woman gets addicted to them. And then they cut the supply of themselves.

RJ: How to they do that?

FJS: By not showing up, by not calling. And Economics 101 teaches us that when you cut the supply, you increase the demand. Well, if you increase the demand you've got control over the price and you can charge any price you want. And, sadly enough, jerks can charge the price of physical abuse, which is something I DON'T support, but sadly, that's how out of control it's gotten.

RJ: So give the free sample, then drive up the demand by cutting of the supply?

FJS: So then what happens is you have a monopoly on her fun and you can charge something you want.

RJ: So how does a guy go about positioning himself this way in a woman's mind.

FJS: You have to train her by your actions that your time is valuable, and she should drop whatever she's doing if you decide to call. Also, her time can really mean nothing to you because you understand that a pretty face is a dime a dozen.

RJ: Shark, how does a guy create that kind of priority? I know that I train guys to create it by linking so much pleasure to her being with them, that she feels compelled to be around them. But what kind of stuff will a jerk do to drive up his price and her interest in him?

FJS: Well canceling dates or not showing up are typical examples, but they follow the Golden Rule.

THOSE WHO
DON'T LOOK HUNGRY GET FED

Nice guys, you see, are always hungry. And the reason they

are always hungry is they don't have any girlfriends. And the reason they don't have any girlfriends is, they're always hungry. So it's a self-fulfilling prophecy.

RJ: Nasty place to be in.

FJS: Right, So the number one thing about jerks is, they do not act hungry, which is why they get girls, so you're on the upward spiral now. So you have to make it seem, and I don't care if you haven't had sex in six months, you have to make it seem that you're not physically attracted to her in any way, and not show any sexual interest in her at all, so that she has the chance to sell herself to you.

RJ: Now, here I have to disagree a bit Shark, cause I think that could lead to her just wanting you to be her buddy or friend. I think you can use language tricks that I teach to implant the ideas of sex in her mind, so she finds herself thinking of you in that way. And then, you can pull back to make her want more. But I agree, you must never appear hungry. And I also think that you have to make sure that you only give out a free sample; the problem with nice guys is they give away the whole store.

FJS: Exactly. To use an example, if you're going to join a bowling league, and they gave away all the trophies the first week, why would you come back? So, if you're going to give away any trophies, make sure you do it at the end of the year, in order to give people an incentive. It's like the stripper... if a stripper comes out completely naked it's no big deal anymore. The reason why strippers are effective is they have that appeal of peeling away their clothes.

RJ: So would you say you can't go wrong by giving too little?

FJS: Yes, Think of it like buying a stock. Women would rather buy a stock that's been dropping in value, with hopes that it will go up if they just stick with it. So, if you're that poor of a boyfriend, she'll hang on cause she's got too much invested in you.

RJ: How would a jerk handle it if a woman tried to switch the tables here and tried to treat the jerk like he was unimportant? For example, if a woman cancels a date with a nice guy he's all understanding, and may even ask if she wants to go another time? How would a jerk handle it?

FJS: First of all, a jerk would maybe remain dead silent on the phone. Two, they are probably already thinking, "she probably think's she's got a better deal somewhere else." So probably, they'd slam the phone down. And that sudden response shows he's maddable. And that's the key, the difference between nice guys and jerks is a jerk will show a woman he can get mad. And he'll either do that by yelling or ignoring her or just, having a fit. The nice guy never gets mad.

RJ: Man, this is sad, but true!!

FJS: Now the nice guy may in fact get mad, but he doesn't show it to the woman. He may get mad to himself or his friends, like he's going to explode on the inside. So you have to cut your fuse, so you aren't waiting to explode. Explode up front so they know what they are dealing with. See, the smartest investors on Wall Street need to know one thing: What's the downside... what could possibly go wrong. Once they know how bad it can get, they're willing to invest more. Therefore, if you spaz out or flip out, even if you slam down the phone, they know, "Hey, that's as bad as it's going to get... I can live with that," so they're going to come chasing you back.

RJ: Versus a nice guy, where the girl doesn't know what might happen.

FJS: Right. That's why at the end of a relationship with a nice guy he hears from her, "I don't know how to tell you this, because I don't know how you're going to respond to it." She doesn't know that this guy can get mad.

RJ: Talk a bit about duck hunting versus duck chasing.

FJS: Most guys act like the hard-core salesman who keeps asking for the order a million times before he gets the sale. I say, if you have to chase the duck you aren't going to catch him. But you sit in one spot, and watch what the ducks do, like where the fly and what their habits are, you can sit still, and even if you have to use a duck call, you can wait for the ducks to fly overhead and then you can shoot them down, and there's really no effort on your part. You're sitting still.

RJ: You know Shark, as I think about it, I think it would be an unbeatable combination for a guy to use what I teach to create incredible states of pleasure in a woman, and then use what you teach to make that so scarce that she's willing to anything.

FJS: Remember, the word addiction derives from the meaning, "not having". The addiction is from not having; if you keep feeding people chocolate cake all day, they're going to get sick of it and you'll have the reverse effect. So you just let them sample the chocolate cake, and then you put it away. Well, you have to be the drug. You create fun, intense highs, and then you pull it away. It's that simple.▼

# Bibliography

Carnes, Patrick, J., Ph.D. The *Sexual Addiction.* Minneapolis, MN: Comp Care Publications, 1983.

Dobson, James, Ph.D. *What Wives Wish Their Husbands Knew About Women.* Wheaton, IL: Tyndale House Publication Inc., 1980.

Mooney, Elizabeth, C. *Men & Marriage: The Changing Role of Husbands.* New York: Franklin Watts, 1985.

Reich, William. *The Sexual Revolution.* New York: Farrar Straus, 1962.

Robbins, Anthony. *Awaken the Giant Within: How to Take Immediate Control of your Mental, Emotional, Physical & Financial Destiny.* New York: Summit Books, 1991.

Robbins, Anthony. *Unlimited Power.* New York: Fawcett Columbine, 1986.

# Recommended Reading

The Social Skills Playbook - Build Self-Esteem, Overcome Fear of Rejection and Get More Dates, by Jim Rohrbach, Social Skills Coach. Send $11.95 (check or money order) to: The Playbook, 2432 West Suite 3B, Chicago, IL 60645-4644, or call (312) 274 3466.

Nice Guys Don't Get Laid by Marcus Melton. $7.95. To order call: 1-800-345-0096.

Ross Jeffries books and audio-tape programs from Straight Forward, 11918 Millpond Ct., Manassas, VA 22111, or call 703-791-6421.

# Index

Addiction, 95
Aristotle, 111
Authority without
    responsibility, 39

Baldwin, James, 132
Banister, Roger, 113
Bentham, Jeremy, 85
Buddah, The, 109

Caesar, Julius, 82
Caveat, Emptor, 93
Checkhov, Anton, 110
Chinese proverb, 51

Discounts, 66-69
Duroucher, Leo, 35

Emotional Nurse, 129
E.R.A., 105-106

F.S. Shark Foundation, 140
Ford, Henry, 112
Fuller, Thomas, 125

German prverb, 27
Glasgow, Ellen, 116
Golden Rule, 58

Jeffreries, Ross, 10, 19, 147-
    51, 153

Kennedy, J. F., 19

Landon, Michael, 141
Lao-Tsu, Tau Teh King, 127
Lee, Gypsy Rose, 104
Lombardi, Vince, 39
Love Collection Agency, 103
Luce, Clare Boothe, 49

Madonna, 106
Maslow, Abraham, 120
Maugham, W. Somerset, 81
Mencius, 115
Mencken, H. L., 99
Minimum/Maximum Theory,
    137

Premiums, 66-69
Prodigal Boyfriend, 32

Robbins, Anthony, 44, 53, 62,
    84, 88
Rue, Joseph, 119
Russian proverb, 77

Shakespeare, William, 96
Stein, Gertrude, 102

Thoreau, Henry David, 111

Wilde, Speranza, 71

# *Thanks again to...*

The Sultans Delight
8108 W. Oakton St.
Niles, IL 60714
Ph: (708) 289-9449
Fax: (708) 518-8443

Kristin Riess
Independent contractor/dancer
(312) 486-4430

Carl's Photography
4207 W. 63rd St.
Chicago, IL 60629
(312) 284-6197

Borderline Productions Inc.
13001 S. Western Ave., 2nd Fl.
Blue, IL 60406
(708) 626-0911

If you would like to order the **How to be the JERK Women Love: Social Success for Men and Women in the 90's** (4) audio-tape program by F.J. Shark, contact us at:
JERK SCHOOL Seminars Inc.
6228 Oakton Street
Morton Grove, IL 60053
708-965-4222

To find out more about the SHARK Report Newsletter
along with all social sexess stories, comments,
and mail listings should personally go to the Shark himself
at the address of:
Thunder World Promotions, Inc.
c/o F.J. Shark
P.O. Box 29122
Chicago, IL 60629